MW01235591

Look Into My Colors

Zach Klein

ISBN: 0692654135
ISBN-13: 978-0692654132

DEDICATION

To my family, who gave me more second chances than I ever deserved and continued to love me no matter what. To the staff in Atlanta that never quit on me. To Rod and Debra, who will always have my gratitude and respect. To Wade. To the Addict.

CONTENTS

One

We pulled up to the hospital and I went inside to be admitted. I sat down on a couch, completely zoned out. I'm sure I had snorted at least several Klonopins before arriving. My dad sat and waited with me. He was calm. I remember him being too calm. The feeling that he experienced could be best described as peace — peace that his wigged out eldest son was finally getting some treatment. He had been begging me for months to go get help, but my arrogance and denial proved to be stronger. We sat there for nearly an hour.

"Zachary, will you please come this way?"

Finally. I'm ready to see what this recovery shit is all about. "Goodbye, Pop." He gave me a quick hug, and then I left with the woman through the self-locking doors. We walked briskly down a long, brightly lit hallway to her desk. She was a highly energetic woman with short spiky hair, and she chewed gum faster and louder than I thought possible. She was thin, fit, and looked tougher than nails. "How are you?" she asked.

"I'm fine, just ready to relax and get a feel for this place."

I didn't say how nervous I was. She was taking a picture of my face and putting a wristband on me with some kind of information. *What in the world did I just get myself into? I thought this was voluntary.*

"Follow me," she wheezed. It was clear that she was a dedicated smoker. I followed her down another hallway until we reached yet another pair of locking doors. Above them in big

1

letters was a sign that said Unit 3. She plugged her key into the doors and they popped open. I took a long look around and saw fifteen to twenty patients, none of whom were my age. They looked old and worn out. We walked up to a counter where several nurses and mental health technicians were working.

"This is Zachary. Is it Zach or Zachary?" she asked quickly.

"It's Zach." She gave my paperwork to one of the nurses behind the counter. "Just try to relax and I'll see you soon," she said in an attempt to boost my mood. Her face was beaming with a smile that gave comfort in a place so foreign to me.

I noticed an old fridge in the corner of the common area. I walked over to it, opened it, and took out several cartons of cranberry juice. Benzodiazepines make the body really thirsty, and I had snorted plenty several hours ago.

There were about twelve comfortable looking chairs in this common area, all connected together in a U-shape. I walked over to one of the tables to see what kind of magazines or books were there. Suddenly, I felt someone looking directly at me. It was that feeling where you know the person wants to say something, but you refuse to look at them because *you* don't want to talk.

He opened his mouth to speak. "Hey son, I'm Mike," the man said. His voice was kind and soothing.

"I'm Zach, nice to meet you."

"What brings you in here?" he asked politely.

I still don't know why I lied to him. I had no reason to lie. *I'm in a mental hospital for God's sake.* Before I could continue the spew of lies, a voice screeched out to line up for dinner. I jumped in line for the cafeteria like I was back in preschool. The tech (our sitter) unlocked the double doors and we started our journey to dinner down a brightly lit maze.

The cafeteria was filled with patients from the different units in the hospital. There was a sitter for each of the units to make sure nobody was assaulted and to call for help if a patient freaked out. The kitchen staff really caught my eye as I went through the meal line. All of them looked tough and desensitized — they had seen it all. One worker stood out to me specifically. His eyes were kind and showed a gentle and simple person who seemed to have real sympathy for the patients. It was either that or he just had pity on us. His job must be awful. I tried to picture myself in his shoes, slaving away for hours in the kitchen prepping boring foods and serving them to depressed and weary patients.

I sat down at an empty table and began to eat. The food was rich and almost too salty. Eventually I would learn that it was filled with carbs and starch to fatten us up. Half of us were extremely malnourished, and the other half could have gone almost a year without eating before they reached a numerical BMI.

"Hey mind if I sit here?" Someone asked me loudly.

"No, go ahead," I replied without missing a beat. He was about forty, redneck as hell, and 6'4" tall. He had curly hair, a leathery face, and looked crazy. If this place needed a picture to advertise, he would perfectly fit the description.

"I'm James man, how you doing man, what you in here for?"

Even though this guy looked terrifying, I liked him immediately. Something about his gangly, hyperactive demeanor drew me in. He didn't seem to care a lick what people thought of him, much less that he was in a mental hospital. I felt my mouth begin speaking my truths. "I'm Zach, nice to meet you," I said firmly. "I'm in here for anxiety issues."

"That's cool man, that's cool…" He looked around wide-eyed, then looked dead at me. "Where's all the chicks man?" he asked. "I ain't seen but a 'bout a couple of 'em."

I laughed internally, finding his question amusing. "Yeah man, I haven't seen a lot of good ones either."

"Well, I'll tell you what, we need to get some good looking chicks up in here," he spat out. "I'm in Unit 3, what unit you in?"

"I'm in Unit 3 as well, just got here about an hour ago." I said.

"No shit? I must have been in my room when you got here. You do know we're in the crazy unit right?"

"What is the crazy unit?" I asked, trying to mask my sudden nervousness.

"The crazy unit is where us misfits go when society don't want us. There's some bat shit crazy people in here, man. That one chick over there talks to the wall. She's cool though," he said, taking a big bite of chocolate cake.

I laughed internally for the second time, but now a grin showed my emotion. He said it with such an easy tone that I really couldn't help myself.

"She talks to the wall?" I asked.

"Yessir, I seen it a couple of times now. Ey, have you seen that chick Melissa yet? She's in our unit too. Man what I would do to that woman."

He went on a ramble of vulgarity, which started to make me

feel uncomfortable. I attempted to steer our conversation away from Melissa.

"What do we do in here?" I asked.

"Well let's see, we wake up around seven, get breakfast, go to group therapy…."

I zoned out and thought about that girl Melissa as he kept rambling on about our daily schedule. *What did she look like? Was she this crazy too?* "…then we get like two hours of free time, then meds, then lights out at ten."

"Do we learn anything? Like does it help?" I asked.

"Help with what?" James didn't seem to think he had any problems or issues that might have landed him in here. I believe he thought that he was perfectly fine.

"Help with using drugs and stuff…I have really bad anxiety, so help with that as well, I suppose."

"Oh yeah, yeah," he said. "Our therapist Kathy is real good at that. She got a bunch of dem quotes and tools and stuff; shit that's supposed to help with anxiety and managing our emotions."

He said it quickly and I could tell it didn't register with him that we are in here for a reason. You don't just wake up one day and sign yourself into a place like this, or do you?

"That's good, I guess I'll meet Kathy tomorrow," I replied, unenthusiastically. "What time is our first group therapy session?"

"Ten o'clock," he said, choking on another bite of cake. "We get breakfast, time for a shower, then medications, and then therapy."

"Unit 3 let's go!" our sitter yelled.

James and I were startled and jumped up immediately. We lined back up at the door and waited for our sitter to go to the front. When we got back to our unit, the sitter unlocked the thick double doors. I darted back to my room to take a shower, filthy from cigarettes and grease. As I was about to lay on my bed and relax, a voice shouted "Meds!" I poked my head out of the door and saw the patients eagerly lining up at the nurse's window. *Their meds must be good*, I said to myself. I walked to the back of the line and waited, and waited, and waited. When it was my turn, the nurse simply smiled and gave me my pills. "Tomorrow you will meet with your assigned doctor, okay?" she said.

"Okay, what's his name?" I asked monotonously.

"Wallace, you will see him around 9:00 a.m."

I walked away and saw James in the back of the line. His height made him look like a giant. He was grinning as usual and motioned for me to come over his way. "Ey man, you get anything good up there?" he asked curiously, like a child.

"I take Klonopin, but that's about it. What about you?"

"I take some Valum and a Lortab every six hours," he replied. "I threw my back out years ago. Damn construction."

I didn't pay any attention to whatever else he rambled about; he just said a Lortab. I felt the calling of an opiate seduction. I hadn't been able to get any the past couple of days and I was craving. It might only be one, but I have to have it.

"Any chance I can get that tab from you?" I asked half jokingly, expecting an immediate rejection.

James gave me a nervous look, then said, "Yeah, I suppose. I'm gonna have to cheek it though."

"What's cheek it mean?" I asked cluelessly.

"Means I act like I'm swallowing it, but hide it in my cheek."

The thought registered to me that I might as well kiss this guy, but I didn't care. I needed that painkiller. It wasn't much, but this craving needed to be at least somewhat satisfied.

"That's cool, I don't mind," I whispered to him. "I really need it man." I tried to act casual and strolled away from the line. My eyes were fixed like a hawk to see if James could pull this off. One by one the patients walked up to the door and took their pills. Finally James walked up, but he immediately started chatting it up with the nurse. When she eventually did give him his pills, he took the glass of water and tilted his head back to swallow. As he was doing so, the nurse looked away to write something on a chart.

He came up to me, looked around, and then handed me a slobbery, blue pill. I could hardly read the inscription, but I knew it was a painkiller — I had taken the blue, magical looking ones like this before. They were not as strong as roxys, but it would have to do. When nobody was watching, I quickly popped the dissolving pill into my mouth, chewed it until it was a paste, then took a big gulp of juice.

It was getting close to eight p.m., which meant we were done for the day and could do whatever for the next couple of hours. James and I went into another common area to make good use of our "free time." In this room were games, puzzles, and pamphlets on mental health issues, such as anxiety, depression, and personality disorders. A few other patients joined our circle for a chat.

Thirty minutes later I remember feeling that creeping buzz. It felt right, and a peace was once again masking itself over my fears and insecurities. We all talked and laughed for a solid two hours before one of the sitters told us it was time for bed.

"Goodnight James," I said with half a grin.

"Night kid, I'll see you in the mornin."

We went our separate ways as the lobby lights faded. Back in my room, I sat at my desk and began to write. Music was a significant part of my life, and now that I was somewhat high, it was the perfect time to get lost in some writing. It just felt right, like that's how it's supposed to be done. Eventually, when my eyes got heavy, I crawled into the thin, cold sheets and began to think. Thoughts of James and Melissa ran in circles through my mind. I still hadn't seen her — I was so preoccupied with learning the rules and then breaking them. James had rambled on about her for so long during dinner that I was expecting a queen.

Thoughts of family then rushed into my head. *Were they scared or hurting? Did they think I was crazy and an addict?* I could feel myself getting angry, so I paused and said a quick prayer. Who knows if I meant it or not. The fatigue was taking over and my mind couldn't process anymore.

My head sunk into the tiny pillow…

"Thump thump…thump thump thump…" I sat up in my bed. *Who could be knocking, it's not even light out yet?*

"Zach? I'm here to check your vital signs," a voice said, still in the dark.

"Okay, I'm up."

A tech walked into my room with a machine with her that took vital signs. "I'm just going to check your vitals okay?" She put a blood pressure cuff around my arm as I fell back into my pillow. I took a deep breath and tried not to be too stiff from the awkwardness of this situation.

"What time is it?" I asked impatiently.

"5:30. First smoke break is in fifteen minutes, if you smoke."

That woke me up completely. She answered my question as if it were asked millions of times. It was good news to me though, as I was smoking at least a pack a day.

Let me take a moment to explain to you the severity of smoke breaks in a place like this. They were very important. They were life and death with some of the patients, including me. We received six to eight smoke breaks each day, depending on the sitter that was on duty. When I first arrived in Unit 3, I had to hand over my packs of cigarettes to the staff. They kept a plastic box behind the nurse's station with all the patients' cigarettes, dip, and cigars. If it was a tobacco product, it was in that box. Every couple of hours a sitter would yell, "Smoke break!" at the top of their lungs. If you ever want to see patients who claim to have physical ailments move, go to a mental hospital and yell it. Patients that were supposedly crippled moved faster than I did.

Next, we lined up at the door leading to the smoking patio and took out our cigarettes from the box. Two smokes was the limit for each break. Depending on the sitter, 2 to 3 smokes was also the limit, and most of the time I tried to take three. After we took out the smokes, we put our packs back in the box, which was then placed in its secure location.

The smoking patio had extremely tall plastic fences. I asked our different sitters several times about what would happen if I broke through them and ran for it. They explained to me that there were several men who would chase patients down if this occurred. I laughed after hearing that. Just picturing my escape made me laugh. Here I am, twenty years old, escaping a mental hospital with several large men chasing after me. As funny as it sounded, I never tried to escape.

Now, back to the story.

"Hey man, how'd you sleep?" asked James. It was clear he did not just wake up as I had.

"I slept alright. The sheets sucked balls though," I replied. "I was cold the entire night."

He burst out laughing. "Yea those sheets ain't right man. You'll get use to 'em."

We talked for the remainder of our first smoke break and then went inside to watch the news. It was now 7:00 a.m. — in thirty minutes we would line up and go to the cafeteria for breakfast. I went back to my room to put on a fresh shirt and jacket for the big occasion. Our journey to the cafeteria that morning was amusing for several reasons. James was once again rambling on about nothing, and Mike, who I mentioned earlier, was telling everyone how happy he was. I was happy too. For the first time in my life, I felt like people understood me. I was around people who didn't judge me, people that liked me for me and didn't care about my flaws or weirdness. Funny how I had to end up in a place like this to get that feeling of security.

When we arrived to the cafeteria, I proceeded to my usual routine of analyzing the kitchen staff. James and I argued over which table to sit at, eventually coming to an agreement and sitting down near the wall of windows where we could see the outside.

"Hey guys, mind if I sit with you?" asked a gentle voice.

James immediately piped up. "Sure, honey, you sit right down." He appeared to have already conversed with her, as they didn't chat like strangers.

They started talking, so I did what I do best and listened, intently. I was trying to hear this beautiful angel. Their conversation lasted for about a minute before she turned to me for a question.

"Hey, I'm Melissa. I don't think I've met you yet?"

"I'm Zach, nice to meet you," I managed to squeak out.

"What are *you* in here for?" she asked me. It seemed like that was the first question patients asked each other when they met. My reply was the same thing I had told James. She nodded, then resumed eating her breakfast. How ignorant and stupid I must have sounded. She was a beautiful woman in her late twenties, and I was the baby of the unit who had just recently turned twenty.

"What are you in here for?" I asked her as charming as possible.

"Well, I have really bad depression, and I'm here because I just couldn't get a grip on it." I nodded and tried to act casual while taking a bite of my powdered eggs. James started up another conversation, but I didn't pay much attention. I was too focused on the softness of her voice. It seemed so kind, gentle, and soothing. *How could a woman like Melissa end up in a place like this? How could it be that a woman this beautiful, so soft-spoken, was suicidal?*

The rest of our breakfast that morning was full of laughs, jokes, and vulgar comments made by James aimed towards

11

Melissa. I stayed out of the vulgarity for the most part but did have some comments to make about some of the other patients in our unit. This one patient, Debra, was suffering from what appeared to be dementia. She was a very sweet woman, but every time we talked I had to reintroduce myself. She called me Jack most of the time, but it didn't bother me much.

After breakfast, it was time for the meeting with my assigned doctor. His name was Dr. Wallace. My first impression of him was not unusual. He was one of those psychiatrists who seemed to practice for the perks and didn't truly know whom he was dealing with or what he was talking about.

I can't remember what Dr. Wallace told me that morning; I tuned out once he opened his mouth. He didn't change my medications except for the Klonopin, which he took me off of almost completely. Besides all that, his personality was arrogant, boring, and not helpful. Imagine how many patients he encountered on a daily basis. He was assigned 4-5 patients from my unit, with four other units to account for. A patient's average stay was between a week and ten days. Then, another round of patients would come in and be treated by this average, incapable, complacent physician.

As you can tell, my "meeting" with Dr. Wallace *really* got under my skin. Thank God it was time for our third smoke break. I went outside where James and Melissa were already puffing away. "That Dr. Wallace is full of it, man," I said loudly to James. I'm sure everybody heard me, because it got quiet on the patio.

"What'd he say to ya?" James asked, laughing with his smoker's cough.

"A whole lot of nothing. I don't think he gives two shits

about the patients here." The look on James face got serious as he started searching for the right words to say.

"Let me tell you something, man," he said. "There are good doctors in here and there are bad ones. You just happened to get a shitty doctor that everybody complains about. Just file a complaint or put in a transfer for a new doctor."

"Nah, I'm not going to be here that long," I said, even angrier than when I first came outside. "I'm pissed man. Why does this place have a doctor who doesn't care about the patients?"

Melissa piped up for the first time. "It's money and politics in here, just like everywhere else," she said, taking a long drag of her smoke. "The community knows him and he has a long list of credentials. Anyhow, who do you think the staff would side with — the psychiatrists or the crazies?"

She made a really good point. I couldn't say much more, so I sat down next to them and took deep breaths of nicotine. *This place is shit*, I thought. *Oh well, at least I have two friendly souls to share my stay with.*

"Time for therapy guys. Hurry up and finish," our sitter hollered to us from the door. "I'll see you guys in there," I said to James and Melissa. Therapy was about to start and if Kathy was really able to help with anxiety and depression, I was going to listen.

Group therapy was split up into two sections. An alphabetical list of last names determined whose group you were in. I happened to be in Kathy's group with James. Melissa was in another therapist's group right next door to our room. The other therapist was in training under Kathy and was extremely good looking. She was young, well educated, and always kind to the patients, including me.

"Alright guys, listen up," Kathy said without an accent. *Where was she from?* I could tell from her voice that she was smart. "Let's start by going around the room and introducing ourselves to each other." One by one the patients went around and gave their name and a specific goal they hoped to achieve during their stay in rehabilitation. While this was going on, James started talking above the other patients, which provoked a strong glare from Kathy.

"Um excuse me? We're talking here," she told James.

"Sorry," he said without remorse. He stopped talking for a minute. It was now my turn to introduce myself. I tried my best to appear smarter than I was because Kathy was quite intimidating. The way she looked at you made it clear that no bullshit would fly past her. I finished my rehearsed speech, hoping to please Kathy.

"Well, thanks for sharing, Zach," she said professionally.

I questioned if what I had just said was stupid or even true. To be honest, I just wanted help with my depression and anxiety. Once my anxieties were managed, I could use drugs the right way; the right way meaning not every day and only a little bit. I was certain that I could use safely once I learned some of their tricks and tips.

Kathy started giving a lecture, which began with a recovery quote from one of her favorite authors. James started talking again to the guy beside him. Kathy stopped lecturing and told him to get out, which James did not like one bit. He muttered something under his breath, I think "bitch," and then stormed out of the room. She apologized to the group and continued on with her speech. If there's one thing I remember from her group sessions, it's the phrase she said so often: "I AM

ENOUGH!" She made sure to repeat it excessively, since most of us had some sort of memory or listening problem.

Later that afternoon, I had one of my only pleasant memories from this place. James and another patient, Ryan, were acting up more than usual. James had taken an extra cigarette and they were waiting for the right moment to smoke it in Ryan's bathroom. I stood guard in the doorway between the room and the bathroom curtain.

"Alright man, I'm gonna light this bitch up," James said to me. "You keep an eye out and after I take a couple of drags Ryan's gonna hit it, then you." I laughed while watching Ryan flip on the air vent switch. James stood on the toilet, lit up the cigarette, and put his face right up to the vent; his eyes were huge. He took a couple of tokes and then gave it to Ryan, who must have weighed about four hundred pounds. He couldn't stand on the toilet, much less stand at all, so he just blew the smoke into it and flushed. He started laughing and handed the smoke to me. James took my place as lookout while I stood up on the toilet to finish off the smoke. I was terrified of getting caught, but the nervousness made the situation exciting. My tokes were huge and gave me a buzz like I had never smoked a cigarette before. We flushed the butt down the toilet and walked out into the hall, laughing hysterically.

"Damn, I got a buzz, boy!" said James. "That's the way to do it right there." His eyes were wide open, and mine were as well. Ryan couldn't stop laughing, which only made me laugh even harder. We looked like a group of boys running from an animal we had just killed. The fact that our next smoke break was in about thirty minutes didn't even occur to us. It was

supposed to be quiet time, and while most of the patients
went into their rooms and slept, us misfits had to find something to do — hence the cigarette. Melissa was in her room
while this all happened, but would soon learn about our
sneaky adventure. I went back to my room and slept for the
remainder of our quiet time.

"Zach! Get your ass up, boy!" yelled James. He was still with
Ryan, who always laughed at whatever James said. I jolted to
an upright position. "Hurry up, man! They started smoke
break ten minutes ago," he yelled, as they hurried outside.

I got out of bed and ran to the smoke patio. Melissa was
sitting on a bench in the corner. Ryan was next to her, and
James sat on a bench with me.

"Hey there, your boys told me all about the smoking," Melissa said to me, smiling. "You guys are crazy!"

"Well, we are in a mental hospital," Ryan barked. "What's
the worst they can do, send us to Unit 5?" His voice was slow,
deep, and raspy, with more than a hint of a southern accent.

Unit 5 was the *real* crazy unit. Patients that had serious disorders, or tended to be violent stayed there. The patients in Unit
3 all had a different idea about what happened in Unit 5.
Some would say they didn't have a caged-in smoking patio.
Others would say they took a smoke break every hour. The
brutally honest patients said that they, "threw their shit and
piss on the walls." However, none of us really knew what it
was like. Each unit is locked up and separated from the others.
All we really knew was our own unit. It was our little space to
seek and find whatever we could.

Melissa kept laughing about our smoking adventure. Ryan
had a way with telling stories that made everyone around him

lean in closely. The way his deep, wide voice dragged over each syllable would always suck us in. Most of the time he spoke in hyperbole, but it made the story better. James would feed off Ryan and then they would laugh. Their laughter was *loud* and always made our sitter and the other patients look over at us. I can only imagine what that group thought — the ones who always sat next to the sitter on the patio because they needed to talk with an *outsider*. Us patients were the *insiders,* and some of us needed emotional comfort. Who can blame them? Everyone in our unit had a different story. Everyone in our unit was unique. Most of the sitters were good listeners, and these patients ate that up as much as they could.

The four of us finished our smoke and went inside to change for dinner. I met Melissa in line and we waited for James, but he never showed up for dinner. It was just Melissa and I left alone to chat casually the entire meal. We talked about our fears, depression, worries, and everything else that we had in common. When we got back to our unit, Ryan was talking to another patient about James. "Yeah, they sent him to Unit 5," Ryan said. I couldn't believe my ears.

"What!" I yelled. "Why?!"

"The nurses told us that he was doing some stuff he shouldn't be doing," Ryan said while rolling his eyes. "If you want my opinion though, Kathy is the one that sent him over there. She does stuff like that around here. If she don't like you, you're gone."

I paused a moment before sitting down next to Ryan. My night had just been ruined. James was all I cared about at the moment. He was one of the coolest guys I'd ever met in my life and now he was gone. "That sneaky woman," I said to myself, "She's good." What she did to James clued me into her capabilities at the hospital. Ryan had been in Unit 3 for the past month and was a sneaky man himself. He kept his mouth shut when the staff was around, but he was listening. He was learning about them the whole time, while they pursued the difficult task of learning him.

Melissa had wandered off when we got back from dinner. She didn't hear the news until I ran up to her and burst it out. "That really sucks. I like James a lot," she said.

"Yeah, I can't believe that…it's all because of Kathy," I hissed. "She decides *everything* in here."

"Well, what can ya do?" she said, shrugging her shoulders.

"I guess nothing now," I sighed. "Hopefully tomorrow we will see him at lunch." Picturing James in Unit 5 made me laugh. He sure will have some people to talk to. If there's one thing he does well, its meet new people.

"Come on, let's go watch a movie," Melissa said, trying to cheer me up. We walked down the hall to the common room where some of the patients were watching an animation. We watched most of the movie together, but I left early to catch my breath. I couldn't focus on the movie. I was too angry with Kathy. *Why would she send James to Unit 5?* He wasn't *that* crazy. He had issues, but not enough to be sent over there! Then it came to me.

Kathy had all the pull in this hospital. She knew all the rotating doctors and they *feared* her. Honestly, I can't really blame them. She was just that kind of woman. When she did something, she did it and did it with purpose. That was great and all, but it didn't take away from the fact that she sent James away from me. Oh well. Tomorrow I'll see James and find out if Unit 5 is as bad people say it is. Hopefully he can still sneak me pills.

Two

Since James was gone, my attention was now pointed in Melissa's direction. I walked outside where she and Ryan were sitting on our usual benches. Each patient had his or her own spot on the smoking patio. It was humorous to me that there were even imaginative territories in a place like this. I suppose it's natural for people to be territorial, and in this place comfort meant everything. Once a patient found a good spot, he or she claimed it every smoke break.

"What's up there, junior?" Ryan asked curiously. I always laughed when he called me junior.

"Eh, not too much. How about you guys? Did you sleep well?"

"Oh yeah, slept like a baby," Ryan said. "What we need is some good coffee in here, junior."

Melissa was still half asleep. I sat down next to her because Ryan was a large man and took up almost the whole bench across from us. "Did you sleep good?" I asked, this time directly towards Melissa.

"Yeah, I suppose," she replied. "I'm not looking forward to my ECT appointment this morning."

"What's an ECT?"

"ECT is Electroconvulsive Therapy. None of my depression medications are working, so the doctors decided that this is my best option. They stick these little pads to your head which gives your brain small seizures."

"That doesn't sound good," I said nervously. "Is that safe? Are there no major side effects from that?"

Ryan spoke up. "I've seen several patients get ECT. Most of the time they are just confused for a few hours, but they get back to normal pretty quick."

I looked at Melissa who was slightly shaken up from the conversation. Her hands were trembling as she brought a cigarette to her lips. "It will work out," I said, trying to sound positive.

"Yeah, I hope so." She didn't sound very confident. "It's really expensive and I've tried everything else. I need this to work." Ryan didn't seem to be concerned. He had already been here for four weeks and seen it all.

The rest of our smoke break was spent in silence. Melissa and I were enjoying each other's company, while Ryan was off somewhere in his head. When break was over, Melissa informed me she wouldn't be coming to breakfast.

"I have to meet with the ECT doctor before the treatment. I'll see you after lunch."

"Okay, sounds good," I muttered sympathetically, as she walked off.

Breakfast that morning was horrible. James was gone, Melissa was gone, and I didn't know what to think about the ECT treatments. It obviously can't be good for you, but if medications don't work then what else can you do? I started to think I wasn't that bad off. Yes, my anxiety could be crippling, but compared to what Melissa was going through I counted myself lucky.

We returned from breakfast and it was time for morning medications. I needed my Klonopin more than usual, so I rushed over to the nurse's station.

"Why did they move James from our unit?" I asked directly to the nurse. She could tell I was in serious need of an explanation.

"Well, I think he was acting out and doing some things he shouldn't have." That was all the information she was going to give me. I took it, along with my little green pill. After walking away, I took notice that Kathy had arrived to the unit. When she saw me looking at her, I gave her the "eat shit" look. I wanted to let her know with my eyes that I knew what was going on. The message was received and she walked away into her office.

Now I'm not positive, but I think the nurse told Kathy about my questioning James's disappearance — group therapy seemed to be directed only towards me. Kathy kept asking me questions as if she was trying to win me over, or at least let me know that she cared. I answered all of her questions and listened closely for her feedback.

Oh, but how good Kathy was at transformation. Somehow she managed to transform my hissy fit into an attitude of optimism, within the hour. Maybe it was the fact that she always kept it real for us patients, or maybe it was her magical powers. She didn't sugarcoat anything and always pointed out our lies and denial. I left group therapy with a more optimistic outlook on my anxiety, even though I was still pissed that she moved James. "I Am Enough," I repeated.

Outside on the smoking patio, there was a group of patients surrounding Ryan, who was telling the story of the century;

he was almost in tears and couldn't stop laughing. When he saw me, he motioned for me to come over. "Junior, junior, come over here," he said wiping the tears away from his squinted eyes. "You gotta hear this." Sitting beside Ryan was his roommate, Geoff.

Geoff was an older black gentleman who had served in the army during Vietnam. He was short and stocky and had developed a stress belly, but that was about the only place on him with fat. He didn't talk very much, but Ryan had told us that Geoff chased people in his sleep. When Ryan would ask him who he was chasing, Geoff would just smile and laugh it off.

At this moment, Geoff was sitting in silence on a bench. He was grinning and smoking away, trying to keep it cool. Ryan told us that while he was in the bathroom, Geoff kept yelling, "Hurry up man, I gotta go." Ryan replied, "I'll be out in a minute, man, hold your britches." Finally, when Ryan was done and walked out of the bathroom, Geoff was standing there. Ryan said, "All yours," to which Geoff replied, "I ain't gotta go no more."

Geoff had shat himself, and Ryan declared that his new nickname would be "Sir-Shit-A-Lot."

I burst out laughing. Poor Geoff! He took it like a champ though, just smiled and smoked his cigarettes. By now the rest of the patients on the smoking patio were looking our way, but we didn't care. We laughed and laughed and cried, and kept saying, "Sir-Shit-A-Lot!" The way it just rolled off the tongue kept us in a frenzy for another ten minutes. Eventually, a tech came over and said to knock it off. "Come on y'all, leave him alone and go line up for lunch!"

We went inside still crying and laughing uncontrollably. Suddenly I remembered that I was going to see James at lunch. *PILL!* My mood got even better, and I made sure to be in the front of the lunch line. Sure enough, by the time I sat down at a table, James was walking in with his unit. He was happily leading the way and talking with everyone like always.

"James!" I yelled out. "What's up man? How's Unit 5 treating you?" He started going through the food line and spoke to me cautiously.

"Hey man, it's not as bad as people say it is. There *are* some crazy ass chicks in there man, not too many lookers though."

"Why did they send you over there in the first place?" I asked immediately, waiting for the necessary information.

"Apparently, Kathy saw how much time we were spending together. She don't think I'm a good influence on you. Plus, she don't like me anyway."

I almost yelled. "I knew it! That woman is sneaky. She's been talking to me all morning in group therapy."

"Yeah, she got me too, brother," he said. "Oh well, it's not so bad over there. The women aren't lookers, but we do get more smoke breaks."

My mind began wandering to a place it shouldn't have. I looked around to see who was watching before I asked James if I could get more tabs from him. He didn't seem bothered by my question.

"Yeah, man. I think our units will get dinner at the same time tonight. I'll try to slip one to you then."

"Awesome, you the man, James." I said, giving him a fist bump.

I finished thanking him repeatedly before a tech told me to go sit with my unit. *Hell, he's going to forget, but it was worth a try.* Man, I missed James. He had a way with strangers and I really envied his personality. The way he was able to talk to anyone about anything made me jealous. Plus, he was giving me opiates, which I loved more than almost anything in the world.

I went and sat down at a table with Ryan. I tried to make conversation, but I kept thinking about James and why he was even in a place like this. Something didn't add up; I needed to find out what it was. Even if James was crazy, he still had a good heart.

When we returned to our unit, I found Melissa sitting in a chair in the common room. I wasn't sure how her procedure went, or if it even worked. She looked confused. The blank stare in her eyes frightened me. I didn't know whether to approach her or leave her alone, but before I had a chance to make up my mind a nurse went over to talk with her, so I darted outside to the smoking patio. I sat next to Ryan and waited to see if Melissa would join us. About five minutes into our smoke break, she walked outside. She came over and sat down next to me, closer than usual. "How are you feeling?" I asked quietly.

"I'm a little dizzy and my head is killing me," she said slowly. Her speech was somewhat slurred and robotic. Ryan was sitting on his bench across from us, alert and attentive to the conversation. He had seen several patients receive ECT therapy and always analyzed them afterwards.

"Wha'd the doctor say? Did the procedure go well?" Ryan asked.

"I guess so. I still have three more treatments to go before I get discharged." Her eyes were glazed over; the blank stare on her face freaked me out — she seemed zombified.

I reached my arm out and gave her a hug. "I'm here if you need to talk about it."

She leaned into my hug. "Thanks. The doctors told me to rest this afternoon and said I should be feeling better by tonight."

"Okay, so I guess I'll see you at dinner?" I asked.

"Yeah, I will be there." She walked inside as Ryan and I sat in silence.

"Are all the patients like that after ECT?" I asked Ryan.

"Most of them." He paused and took a big drag from his cigarette. "Many times I see patient's personalities change afterwards. They ain't the same anymore." His answer scared me. I could definitely tell that Melissa's personality had changed, but I didn't want to believe it would last like Ryan had said.

"It seems like her depression is worse than before," I told him.

"Yeah, that's what it looks like. You never know, junior. She's still got three more treatments."

"That's true, hopefully she will be feeling better by dinner. I want the old Melissa back."

I finished my smoke and went inside to my room. This whole situation wasn't sitting well with me, so I opened my journal and began expressing my worries through lyrics. It was a depressing song, but if my memory serves me correctly, it was called, "Beautiful Eyes." After a short period of somber writing, a tech came into my room and told me it was time for group therapy. I went, but I couldn't focus. Melissa was all I had on my mind.

When we lined up to go to dinner several hours later, Ryan was in an elevated mood. He could always make me laugh if I was gloomy; I couldn't help but smile when he was around.

"Hey boys," I heard a voice say from behind me.

Immediately recognizing the voice, I turned around and saw Melissa walking towards the line. She looked much, much better. Her eyes didn't have a blank stare and her voice was perky again.

"Hey there," I said with a large smile. "You look good! How did you sleep this afternoon?"

"I feel a lot better, thanks. My head doesn't hurt as bad and I'm not nearly as groggy," she replied, moving the back of the line to join me.

"That's great! I'm so glad. I was worried sick about you this afternoon."

"Aww that's sweet," she said, reaching out and touching my arm. The tech opened the doors and we went to dinner. As soon as we got to the cafeteria, I started looking for James. By the time I sat down at a table with my tray, Unit 5 was entering the cafeteria and James was leading the way. I walked up to the line and pretended to get a juice, or something like that.

"Hey man," I said to James.

"What's up boy? How's everybody doing over there?"

"Well, Ryan is great, and Melissa is recovering from her first ECT treatment."

"Damn, that sucks," he said. "Tell her I hope she feels better."

"I will for sure." I leaned in a bit closer, "You bring me a tab?"

"You know I did," replied James, without missing a beat.

I laughed, not expecting James to be so carefree in his giving. It was truly a gift without any reciprocity expected. He reached across the juice bar and grabbed a napkin. He put the tab into the napkin and then put it on my tray.

"You the man, James," I said quietly. "How long do you think you'll be here?"

"Well, they told me I can go home tomorrow afternoon sometime. Doc says I'm doing good and there's not much else they can do for me here."

His news broke my spirit. I felt like James had been more of a friend to me than anyone I'd ever known. More importantly, he made me feel like I wasn't alone. He accepted me for who I was.

"Damn, James," I said. "Can I get your number tomorrow so that we can stay in touch?"

"Of course, man. When you get out of here you can come down to my lake house and party with these college chicks."

I laughed. "That sounds real good man. I gotta get back to my unit, but I'll see you at lunch tomorrow."

"Alright'y then," he replied.

I walked back to my table where Ryan and Melissa were laughing it up. "How's James doing?" Melissa asked.

"He's actually doing well. His doctor said he can go home tomorrow."

"Oh, shit!" said Ryan. "They're releasing another one of us into the world. Lord help us all."

"Good for him," Melissa said. "He didn't seem like he was that bad off anyway."

"Yeah, I know what you mean. I think he's going to be alright."

We finished dinner and went back to our unit. I went straight to my room and took out the tab from the napkin in my pocket. "Wow, you're beautiful," I said to the blue pill. I put it in the pocket of my small brown journal, then put the journal in my jacket.

It was time for a twelve-step meeting in the common area. Several men and women came to the hospital twice a week to lead these meetings. They spoke mostly about alcohol, which struck me as funny, since I was in there for anxiety and depression. I didn't listen to a word throughout the meeting. I was just waiting for my Klonopin and the gorgeous blue pill I had in my pocket. As soon as the final prayer was said and the meeting was over, I went back into my room to do business.

I closed the bathroom curtain and turned on the faucet. Then I crushed the pill in some paper with my pencil. I rolled up the paper and snorted. A feeling of satisfaction hit my brain.

The drip tasted great. The clogged nose felt great. The buzz was coming on strong. I cleaned up the evidence and went to take my other medications. My buzz was setting in by now and with the Klonopin kicking in shortly, I would be feeling halfway high.

Melissa and Ryan were already smoking outside. I rushed out to the patio to join them. I sat down next to Melissa and jumped in on the conversation without knowing what the hell they were talking about. All I knew was that I was at peace. I was not worried or anxious. I was satisfied being locked up in this place. Besides, I was with the people that made me feel normal.

Then I remembered — no more blue pills from James. Damn.

The next day at lunch I had to say goodbye to James. He gave me his number and said to call him so we could party. What a unique and special person he was. James was friendly, outspoken, kind, and a little bit crazy. His weirdness and simplicity were what drew me in. It takes one to know one, I suppose.

Three more days went by in Unit 3, and I continued to meet with my doctor. I was taking 3 mg of Klonopin at the time, but he said that he was going to lower it to .5 mg twice a day. However, he told me this the day before I was discharged. In addition to the doctor visits and therapy sessions, I grew closer to Melissa. She continued to receive her ECT therapy, gradually slipping away with each treatment. She talked slower and things didn't seem to bother her as much anymore.

One afternoon she was standing at the end of a hall, her bright blue eyes just staring at me. She kept staring, so I walked up to her and asked if she was okay.

"No," she said. "I'm not okay."

We prayed together, but my prayer was not a true request for God's help or mercy. It was the instinctual response, the last resort option, the only thing left to do.

On the day of my departure, Kathy told me I had to fill out a crisis plan. She put more of an emphasis on anxiety rather than substance abuse, but probably because I was still so secretive about it. Unit 3 was also a psychiatric unit, not a detox unit.

I hurried through the paperwork so I could get the hell out of there. I hadn't smoked pot in a week and was eager to get high. Melissa informed me that she would be leaving two days later. She wrote me a nice goodbye letter, which contained her number and email address. "I'm having a party when I get out of here — you, Ryan, and James are all invited." I laughed and said I'd be there. Several of the patients, including Ryan, wished me farewell.

I remember walking out of Unit 3 through the thick double doors. Melissa sat in the common room and watched me leave. She didn't look happy or sad — she just watched me. Finally, when the doors had shut, a tech walked me out to the waiting room.

Pop was waiting in the lobby to take me home. We talked very little on the way to his house in Greenville. He asked me when I would be ready to go back to my apartment in Central. "This afternoon," I replied. When we got to the house, I gave mom a hug and said goodbye to my brothers, then left. I called my roommate to tell him I was on the way home.

"Good, how are you feeling?" He asked.

"Oh, I'm fine. Feeling good."

The inner debate on whether or not I should get high only lasted a few minutes. My conscience was very loud, but the weed won. Damn it felt good to smoke again.

A few days passed as I unsuccessfully tried to adjust to .5 mg of Klonopin twice a day. My body felt like shit, worse than before going to the hospital. To make things worse, the next appointment with my regular psychiatrist was not for three weeks, but I *needed* more benzos.

I called the same hospital and told them what was going on. Apparently, I freaked out the receptionist because she told me to come back. *Come back?* Her advice didn't upset me. Why? Was it because I enjoyed being around fellow addicts and my own kind? Was it because I didn't have to worry about anything on the inside? Was it because I felt like people gave me attention?

Telling my roommate about going back to the hospital was the only difficult part, because it was embarrassing. He didn't say much, not knowing what to think of the situation. He had personally witnessed my spiral of drug abuse since the start of the semester: the weed, the cocaine, the opiates, the Klonopin, and of course, tons of alcohol. It was clear from *his* perspective, I needed help.

I drove straight to the hospital without stopping. Once I got there, I filled out the paperwork, put on another wristband, and skipped the assessment. Kathy must have known about my return because she didn't look the least bit surprised to see me when I walked through those double doors again.

"Are you going to listen this time?" she asked.

"I'm going to try," I mumbled without reassurance.

I looked around to see if I recognized any patients from a week ago. There were a couple of familiar faces, but a lot of new ones as well. A familiar voice shouted my name from down the hall. "Junior!" *Oh shit, it's Ryan.* "What the hell happened?" he asked.

I hung my head. "I uh…I really don't know." It was hard to look him in the eye.

"Well, you're going to get it right this time, junior," he said with confidence. "Do you know who you're rooming with yet?"

"No, I literally just got here," I spat out.

"Ah ha…you're going to room with me, junior. I've had a room to myself for about a week now. I'll go talk to Kathy and tell her to stick you with me. You better believe I will set you straight junior." I laughed and watched big Ryan move with a purpose up to the nurses' station and ask for Kathy. She looked annoyed but came out from an office anyway.

"What is it, Ryan?" she asked.

"Now Kathy, junior here needs a good roommate. I think you ought to stick him with me."

"Oh really?" Kathy put her hands on her hips.

"Yes, Ma'am," replied Ryan. "I'm going to give him a talking to and set him straight."

Kathy laughed, "I'll see what I can do."

About five minutes later, a tech told me to go to room 502. Ryan was sitting on his bed with an oxygen mask in his nose. He gave me a slow, deep grin, then put his arms behind his head. He waited to say anything until the tech walked out of the room. "Well well well, junior. Sit down and tell me what happened," he said, patting my bed. Trying to come up with a logical explanation stupefied even myself.

"Damn…well, I got back to my apartment and tried to get used to the .5 mg of Klonopin. I couldn't do it man; I felt terrible. This morning when I called and told them what was going on, they recommended coming back. That stupid, stupid doctor! What the hell is wrong with him? He doesn't have a clue how bad my anxiety is."

Ryan took a big breath from his mask. His oxygen machine was humming softly in the background.

"I think you should talk to Kathy and ask for a different doctor. There are a couple good ones in here."

"I'm definitely getting a new doctor. I don't think I can take one more meeting with Dr. Wallace, that idiot."

He took another deep breath. "You have to fill out a form from the nurses station and they will put it in your file. It shouldn't take long; it's only a couple of questions."

"Gotcha. Alright, I'll be back. Gotta take care of that before I lose it." I rushed to the nurse's station because it was almost time for dinner. Ryan was correct about the form being so simple.

1) *Who is/was your doctor?*

2) *Why do you feel like you need a different doctor?*

I wrote fast and with anger. My answers made it quite clear that I wasn't happy with the first doctor they assigned me. Kathy called me aside after dinner and informed me that she had read my request form and would give me a different doctor. I spun around to go to my room.

"Zach…"

I turned around, "Yes?"

"I'm glad you're back. I knew you were not ready to leave, but we have a lot of work to do this time."

"Yeah, I know. Thanks Kathy." I smiled as she walked away.

It was odd that I felt no more anger towards Kathy. She really did care for me, but was I ready to move on with my life? As bad as it sounds, I felt relieved to be back in Unit 3. No judgment was being passed on me — only tactical advice and tools from the staff to help us deal with real world problems on real world time. I was not "weird" in here, but normal and understood. It was the outside that was the weird place — people faking, hiding secrets, spinning lies.

I spent the rest of that night meeting a few new patients and explaining myself to the old ones. This itself consumed most of the evening. The next morning, I woke up feeling like a new person. I used my time during breakfast to focus on what I should say to my new doctor. I rehearsed how the conversation would go, what I should say, and how much of my *real* drug use would be appropriate.

Shortly after breakfast, it was doctor time. I waited eagerly for my name to be called. "Zachary?"

"Yeah, that's me." I stood up quickly and walked with him to a small office. He looked like your average Joe. He was good-looking, thin, and in his forties.

"I'm Dr. Gibson. How are you feeling this morning?" His voice was quiet but alert.

"Doing okay, I'm a bit anxious. Dr. Wallace cut my Klonopin down to .5 mg twice a day, which I don't think was a good idea. That's why I'm back here."

He wrote on my chart for a moment. "So you think that's the main problem, your anxiety?"

"I know that's the problem," I replied, twisting my hands together and looking around at the walls.

"Do you feel like the Klonopin has been working for your

anxiety?" I thought very carefully for a moment before answering. "It works okay, but I use to take Valium, which worked a lot better."

"Why do you think that is?" he asked, jotting down more notes.

"I don't know exactly, it just seems to relieve my anxiety without making me feel loopy." That was a lie. I liked Valium better.

I cringed awaiting his response.

"Fair enough, we can try that. I'm going to keep the Lexapro and the Temazepam where they are." He paused for a moment. "You know the marijuana is not helping with your anxiety. You're actually making it worse." He waited for me to speak, but I simply nodded my head. "We're going to keep you here a little bit longer this time," he added. "I think we let you go a little too early last week."

"That's what Kathy said," I blurted out.

"Alright, well I can see you are pretty anxious. I'll have one of the nurse's give you a diazepam. Let's try a 10 mg at breakfast, one in the afternoon, and one at bedtime."

"Thanks doc," I sighed. "I'll work harder this time. I need to get better."

We ended our meeting and I went back to my room extremely satisfied about getting some relief. When Ryan asked how the meeting went, I replied, "Couldn't have gone better."

He pinched his lips together, "I'm not surprised, junior. Gibson is a popular one among the patients. Most of them really like him."

After taking a much-needed Valium, I spent the rest of the day enjoying my lack of anxiety. Later that night I called Melissa and told her about being back in Unit 3. She was worried, but glad that my medications were getting situated again. We talked for nearly an hour before a tech kicked me off the phone.

"I miss you," I told her.

"Miss you too. Goodnight." I hung up the phone.

Three

Ryan had already been in the hospital for several weeks when I first met him. Now that we were roommates, I would truly start to understand more about him. We discussed the past, but most of our conversations were about present situations, like his mother. She had severe dementia and was in the hospital. When they would talk on the phone, she would always ask him where he was and when he was coming to see her. Ryan's response became a routine and each time he would say the same thing. The more that cycle went on, the more hopeless he felt.

Ryan was just a big teddy bear. He had two or three chins and his deep southern voice always made me laugh. The way that he changed the dynamics of his voice when telling a story was always entertaining. He loved to call me junior; it just sounded right when he would say it. Nobody else could have gotten away with that, but he did. It sounded like a father talking with his son and giving him advice; just simple conversation. Many times in the afternoon, we would sit on our beds and talk about everything we could possibly think of.

One of the best memories I have of Ryan was the game he would make me play before I could go smoke. He'd have me make the bed military style, and then he would wobble over and throw a nickel on it. If it didn't bounce he told me to make the bed again. After three days of practice, I improved just enough to meet his standards.

On the morning of my fourth day back in Unit 3, Ryan told me that we were getting two new patients in our unit. He always knew when patients were coming and going. It was actually really impressive. Sure enough, after lunch two guys were admitted.

I waited until they came into the common area before I introduced myself. Cal was twenty-three, and he was at an in-between stage. By that I mean in-between different jails. He was in the army and had just recently returned home from a tour in Iraq. There were several scars on his face, and he had a shaved head. His appearance was scary, but he seemed relaxed in our environment. Tim, on the other hand, was seventeen, and he was sent over from the adolescent unit. I forget why that was, but it was unusual nonetheless.

Shortly after meeting Cal and Tim, we all went outside for our after lunch smoke break. Ryan started asking Cal questions about the war, what he had experienced, and how he got the scars. His response was that he was out at a bar one night, still in army mode. It had only been a few weeks since he had returned home. Cal said he got into an argument with three other guys at the bar and gave them his address so they could come get some.

Cal drove straight home and grabbed his sawed-off shotgun and a 9 mm pistol. Ten minutes later, he looked out the window and saw two cars drive up. He walked outside and, without saying a word, opened fire on them both. The cars sped off and the police showed up shortly after. "I didn't aim for the guys in the car," he said. "If I wanted to kill them, I would have." The judge gave him some grace due to his service and PTSD. I don't remember how much jail time he was looking at, but it wasn't a large amount considering he unloaded a sawed-off shotgun in one hand and a 9mm in the other.

His story consumed our entire smoke break and none of us were even smoking. I quickly huffed down a cigarette and walked inside, still thinking about it. Back in my room, Ryan was sitting on his bed with his oxygen tubes in his nose.

"Can you believe all that stuff Cal was saying?" I asked Ryan.

"Actually yes, junior…that kid looks like he has been through a ton of shit."

"Yup. I feel bad for him."

"Nah, don't need to feel bad for him. He's a strong young man and he'll get through it," he replied. "I do wish we would give better care to our veterans when they come back home. He was was out there getting shot at and blown up."

I could tell that Ryan didn't like talking about it, so I quickly changed the subject. "What do you think about that Tim kid?" I asked. "He seems like a cocky little shit to me."

"He's just young, junior. It might just be a defense mechanism. He's probably scared to death." Ryan was probably right — Tim actually made me think of myself.

"So, are you going to recreational therapy?" I asked.

"No. I never go. I did maybe once or twice when I first got here, but it's a bunch of kid games and stuff I don't care for."

"I gotcha. Well, I'll see you when I get back then."

Recreational therapy consisted of adult patients coloring, working puzzles, painting, and playing word games. You would think that it was a therapy consisting of physical activity. It wasn't. More often than not, the patients were on new or different medications, and elevated blood pressure and increased heart rate could cause problems. But, what really sucked was the piano in the corner of the gym, which I always asked to play. The therapist told me I could play it in the last five minutes of the session, but that rarely occurred due to all the arguing and chaos. By the time recreational therapy was done, we were just figuring out how to do the activity! But that's why I went. I laughed more in that gym than I ever had before. The therapist that led it was always stressed out. She did not seem like a people person, but she did have unbelievable patience. I assumed that was a necessity when working with people like us.

When we got back from recreational therapy, it was time for my afternoon Valium. Snorting the pill would give me a better buzz, so I decided to cheek it. I ran back to my room and closed the bathroom curtain. Ryan was sitting on his bed and heard me crushing up the pill.

"Junior, you gotta quit doing that...you're not going to get any better if you keep shoving pills up your nose."

I stopped crushing for a moment. "Yeah, I know man...I won't do it anymore after today."

"We'll see about that," he replied.

I flushed the evidence down the toilet and fell on my bed. *Only a few more days*, I thought to myself. *A few more days.*

I was supposed to leave after one week. Well, at least that's what Kathy said. When day seven came, and she told me I was going to be staying a little bit longer, I almost lost it. The thought of being sent over to Unit 5 kept me from doing anything too stupid. Even Ryan noticed my withdraw and impatience. He mentioned a few times that I needed to get my shit together and never come back to this place. "Damn right," I told him, with anger slowly rising up inside of me. *I will never come back to this place. Forget Kathy, forget therapy, forget all of it.*

Then that happy day came. Naturally, I was in a good mood. Nobody had ever been in a bad mood on the day they were released. If they were, they usually didn't leave. Ryan and I had a good talk as I was packing my clothes, journal, and medications.

"Junior, you're a good kid, and I love you like one of my own. I'll beat your ass if you ever come back here."

"You got it, Ryan," I said with a smile.

"I mean it junior, take care of yourself."

"I will, promise man."

I gave big Ryan a hug, and he clung on to me for a minute, which made me tear up. I had to pull away because I didn't want to think about it anymore. I kept telling myself not to think, just leave.

Kathy pulled me aside and told me to continue progressing in my recovery and to not stay stagnant. She said a few other things, but I was more focused on passing through those locked doors and getting to my car. Then that lady came to get me; the wiry one who always chewed gum and walked fast. I greeted her with a big smile. She asked how I was doing and if I was excited to go home. I said yes, of course. It had been a long twelve days.

When we got to the exit, I wasn't exactly sure if I could just walk out the door. Eventually, I got a clue and walked outside with my bag in one hand and my keys in the other. It was sunny outside with a slight breeze and a nice temperature. I sighed, smiled, and unlocked my white Aurora, putting the sunroof back and turning the radio on blast. It felt weird to be driving again and able to do whatever my heart desired. For a brief moment I forgot about wanting to get high again. This freedom felt good enough for now, and I wanted to show my parents that I was doing better. *Stay focused*, I told myself. Sober would have been a better word, but focused was on my mind.

I drove back to my apartment early the next morning. The fall semester was just about halfway done and I had already missed a solid two weeks of classes. *Take it slow, think positive, and don't get high,* I told myself.

A full two day's worth of classes went by before I smoked weed again. This time though, I told myself that I would not smoke during the day, and there would be a limit to how much I spent on it. My plan worked for about two weeks. During that time I tried to make up all the missed work, but it was too overwhelming. I withdrew from my classes and planned to start over again in the spring.

As depressing as it was, I tried to think of the positives, like getting a job, recording more music, working out again, anything. Music was my life, but music was also one of the driving forces behind my drug use. The weed made my music sound better, the cocaine made me perform better, and the benzos helped me relax once I was done recording. Oh, and popping some painkillers made me happy about my music. If I couldn't have those drugs, then no music. I couldn't, it just wasn't the same. It didn't sound the same, it wasn't enjoyable, and I hated it. *If I hate making music, then what am I on this earth for?* My life came crashing down with this realization, which led to nothing productive for the next few weeks.

Occasionally I'd drive from Central to Greenville for some landscaping jobs, but other than that I'd stay in the apartment and work on my tunes. I was having fun again, I was happy again, but I was also using a lot of drugs again. My dealer always had people over at his house doing drugs, so I spent most of my nights over there. Twice I mentioned going to the hospital for anxiety and depression. "Why do you keep going back there?" he asked. It was a really good question. Not once did he mention the drugs he was selling me, and not once did I mention the various drugs I was buying from him. It was the elephant in the room that was not discussed. *Why was I doing this to myself?* He did make a valid point. It seemed like going to the hospital was actually making everything worse. But in fact, the battle had just begun.

The semester was nearly over and I had absolutely nothing to show for it except for student loans and three trips to a mental hospital. This depressing truth threw me into a hellacious week of binging, and I found myself back in Unit 3 for the last time.

Everything was different.

Ryan was still there, but he was a completely different person. He barely said a word to me when I walked in — just shook his head and wobbled off. Kathy was also upset when she saw me walk through the doors. I could feel myself becoming a regular. The staff knew my name very well by now. Even the kitchen crew called me by Zach.

I was assigned the same doctor as the last time, who immediately asked what happened. The question did not bother me at all. It was his tone that bothered me. His voice was no longer concerning; it was almost demanding. That *really* freaked me out. *What was going on with everyone? Why were they acting like this?*

I felt like even the people trying to help me had given up on me. Most of the patients I'd gotten to know had been discharged. There were only two patients left from my second stay, and Ryan and Mike were the only patients left from my first stay. Since I didn't like change, and since Ryan now despised me, I distanced myself from nearly everyone.

My last time in Unit 3 could best be described with one word: anger. It started off with a phone call to my roommate in Central. I wanted to check in and let him know what was going on. During our conversation he told me that he was moving out of the apartment after Christmas break. The news threw me into a completely disoriented state.

On several other occasions I made phone calls to friends and family members, but only to rage on them with my hurtful and provocative words. Several days of this caused Kathy to pull me aside and tell me she knew what was going on. The nurses and techs heard a lot more than what you might think, and eventually the details of my phone conversations spread to her and my doctor. This made me paranoid about being sent to Unit 5, so I immediately cut off all contact with everyone on the outside of the hospital as well.

My inner frustrations eventually came out in a group therapy session. Kathy paid close attention to my speech, and a day or two after my rant she told me that I needed to go to out-patient therapy after being discharged. For out-patient therapy, you go to the hospital (different building) and participate in group therapy sessions, but at the end of the day you could go home.

I didn't have many options left. I called my dad and explained to him the situation with my roommate. I was mostly at a loss, so I simply asked if I could move back in with them for a while. I'm sure Kathy also talked to him, because he agreed to let me stay at his house under certain guidelines and conditions, one of which being that I participate in out-patient therapy. His other conditions included staying clean, getting a part-time job, and attending narcotics anonymous meetings regularly. I was slightly hesitant on the phone, but I agreed to follow the guidelines. Two days later I left unit three for the last time.

Goodbye Unit 3

Four

It was a dark day when I moved out of my apartment in Central. I was worn out, exhausted, and agitated about my living situation. Moving back into my parent's house was an absolutely terrible experience. I really despised the idea of being snooped on, policed, or held accountable. Remembering that out-patient therapy started on Monday made me even more aggravated, and a cycle of bitterness and addiction was in full force.

I had to make sure my bottle of Klonopin was with me when I arrived at out-patient therapy on Monday. I even snorted a couple before it began. The long walk into the different building at the hospital didn't sit right with me either, because change sucked. Change made me feel disoriented and confused.

I looked around for anyone that had been in Unit 3 with me. There was only one person I recognized — Braden.

Braden was in his early thirties, had few teeth (so he rarely smiled), and a big beard. He was really quiet in Unit 3 and we had only spoken a few times. But, since I didn't know anybody else, I went up to him and asked how he was doing. To my surprise, he seemed a bit more talkative and alert than I remembered.

We hit it off right away, mostly conversing about the patients who had been in Unit 3 with us. Braden had formed what seemed to be a mutual "friendship" with a girl in the unit.

That wasn't hard for me to believe; every time I saw him in the common room, they were together. They were both melancholy, spoke few words, and seemed to hate everything except each other's company.

We finished our conversation and then went inside to start group therapy. Afterwards, we stayed out in the parking lot and continued talking. We exchanged numbers and said our goodbyes for the day, but thirty minutes later I got a text from him — a lot of texts from him. He was much more talkative via texting than in person, which I thought was strange. Regardless, we texted on and off that afternoon and picked up right where we left off in the morning at group therapy.

Our personalities were very different, and I think that's why we hit it off so well. I was always smiling and trying to give him positive feedback on whatever he would ask, which was usually about that girl. He was insecure about the situation and wanted to know what he should say, if he should call her, did she like him, did she not like him, and other adolescent questions like these. I was just desperate for friendships and trying to fill this lonely void in my soul. I was equally as insecure as he was, but my way of showing it was by trying to fix everything.

The following week Braden asked if I wanted to go to his house one night, and then go to group therapy together in the morning. I thought it sounded like a good time, so on that Monday night I drove down through the country to his house. When I got there, it looked like an average house in an average neighborhood. Braden came out and greeted me, and then we went inside. After a short tour of his house, he approached his pill cabinet.

"So what kind of meds are you taking?" I asked.

He smiled, showing his missing teeth. "Well, I take an anti-depressant, Tramadol, Ativan, and Lortabs for my back. What about you? What do you take?" he fired back.

"I take Lexapro, Restoril, and Klonopin. I was on Seroquel but that made me sleep fourteen hours, so I'm just taking those three now."

He nodded his head like he was impressed — his lower lip rose above above the upper lip. Then he asked me if he could have one of my Klonopins. I seized the opportunity and said, "Yes, but only if I can have one of those Lortabs."

Braden laughed, "Mmmm…okay, I guess."

We traded pills like a couple of middle-schoolers trading sack lunch desserts. Then we walked outside on his porch to relax. Braden started rolling up some cigarettes. "So you think I should call her?" he asked.

"When was the last time you talked to her?"

He paused, "I called and texted her a few days ago, but she only texted me back once saying hey."

I thought for a moment of something wise to say. "I would wait for her to call you. She might be getting settled in or whatever. You should wait another day or two before you contact her again."

Braden didn't seem to like that idea, but he nodded and kept rolling cigarettes. After an awkward silence he went inside to the kitchen and started looking for ingredients, like he was going to cook something.

"What are you doing?" I asked.

"I'm going to cook," he replied. It took me a minute to realize he was talking about meth.

I wanted to walk out the door, but the curious side of me wanted to watch the process. He took out the various ingredients, grabbed an empty soda bottle, and walked back out to the porch. The whole process looked like a chemistry project, not nearly as scary or dangerous as you see on the news.

"Follow me," he said.

We walked outside and went through his backyard towards a small shed. Braden worked his magic and finished the process. We walked back up to the house. The finally results were these bluish-purple chunks of what looked like powder.

I just kind of shook my head and did the lower lip above the upper thing. He took the chunks out of the jar and asked if I wanted to smoke a little.

"Hell no," I said.

"Well, you can snort it too, if that's what your afraid of," he said, laughing. I contemplated the idea for what seemed like an eternity.

"Just a little line," I said.

The after-burn was unlike any burn I had ever felt before. It was much more powerful and almost knocked me off my feet. "Damn!" I yelled. Braden just stood there smiling; he knew it was the good stuff. He looked around for a small light bulb to make a bowl.

A feeling hit me out of nowhere. "I feel good, man. That's not what I thought it would be," I told him.

He didn't respond, just nodded his head. The high was creeping up on me now. I felt focused, alert, powerful, and in need of something to do. "Let me get one of those rolling papers and tobacco," I said. He handed me some papers and tobacco.

We sat out on the porch and rolled cigarettes for at least three hours. I must have smoked close to a hundred. I specifically remember not being able to satisfy my nicotine craving. Chain smoking cigarette after cigarette after cigarette just would not satisfy. I needed something else to do, and fast. There was a knife on table that reminded me of my whittling days as kid. Braden enjoyed carving as well, so we sat in his living room whittling and listening to old records as the night grew late. Occasionally we would stop what we were doing to ingest more of that purplish monster. The new burning sensation felt unbelievably good. I just couldn't get enough. That night I popped more painkillers, snorted more benzos, and smoked four packs of cigarettes. More.

That's what I needed.

More.

Five

The Christmas spirit was now in full swing.

Out-patient therapy would continue one more week before taking a short break for the holidays. My friendship with Braden continued, but it was more or less for the fact that misery loves company. He still frequently asked for my advice on his girl, but the same answers always came out of mouth, and our misery continued.

The following Thursday, after my second week of out-patient therapy, I went down to Braden's house again. My intentions were quite specific this time. My hair was greasy and long, my face was thin, and my attitude was manic.

"We gonna cook tonight?" I asked excitedly.

"Yeah, but you're going to have to buy the ingredients tonight. I've bought my limit for this month."

We picked up the necessary ingredients and went back to his house to begin cooking. On this visit, I was far more eager for his tedious work to be complete. My eyes were wide with excitement, like a child in a candy store. Snorting was always fun, but smoking it sounded like it would be that next level, and I eventually gave in to the temptation. That punch-you-in-the-face feeling felt even better than the first time.

We whittled, rolled cigarettes, and listened to old records. The knife slipped while I was carving and it cut my index finger to the bone. Blood gushed everywhere.

"Braden! Shit, man, get a towel! I cut myself bad." I ran to the bathroom and quickly washed my finger out with soap, but the blood continued to pour out and the throbbing began.

"What the hell happened?" Braden asked.

"I don't have a clue. The knife just slipped."

"Keep it under the water. I'm gonna go find some super glue," he said, laughing.

Braden, who was in no rush, walked leisurely into the kitchen and began searching for some superglue. After what seemed like an eternity, he found some glue and poured it all over and inside the wound. It worked like a charm. I figured it was a good idea to stop whittling; my finger hurt like hell and I was sobering up from the pain.

The next morning my hands were sore, hurting beyond all reason from the hours and hours of whittling. My index finger was now covered in tape, and I didn't dare take it off to look at the damage.

"Alright'y man, have a great Christmas. I'll see you in group therapy after the holidays, right?" I asked rhetorically.

Braden, who was laying on a mattress, replied, "Yeah yeah, I might be there."

"You better be. I'll keep in touch with you." With that, I left Braden's house to spend Christmas with the family.

My relaxing holiday was spent snorting Valium and Klonopin, trying not to flip out from the lack of access to my drugs of choice. My emotions were changing left and right, up and down, leading to a personal hell of darkness and fog. This relentless cycle of anger and craving left me without a single moment of peace.

I think I was in a bad mood because of Braden. He texted me on multiple occasions over the holidays saying that he was going to kill himself, and that really freaked me out. I called the hospital, they called the police, who then called me and asked what was going on. I wasn't trying to get him in trouble, so I told them as little as possible. I sent Braden numerous texts in the following two days to see if he was all right. He never responded, and I eventually gave up. It was a frustrating situation for numerous reasons.

My cravings only grew bigger and stronger. In an attempt to ease these urges, I snorted nearly a mountain of Klonopin and Valium. It only made things worse, and I ended up getting into a fight. The actual blows were a blur, but when I came out of my benzo blackout, there were several police officers questioning me. They pointed out my black eye and asked for my side of the story. Then the medics took my blood pressure and asked me to come with them to the hospital.

"Can I smoke?" I asked them.

"No, you can't smoke at the hospital," a medic replied.

"Well then, I'm not going."

They kept asking me to go with them but I refused, promising to call my place in the morning. Eventually they left, no charges were filed, and a phone call was made the next morning to my friends at the hospital. This time during the phone assessment, my meth binge was leaked out with confidence.

"If you feel like you should come in for an assessment, then let's go ahead and get that set up for today," a lady said through the phone. A brief pause turned into an awkward silence. *Do I really want to go back there? How long are you going to do this?*

I let out a long, defeated sigh before replying, "Sure, I'll come in today." Since I already planned on being admitted again, I went ahead and packed my clothes and medications. Yes, I went back, but they did not send me to Unit 3 after admission. They sent me to Unit 6. "Unit 6 is a dual-diagnosis unit," was the response to my questioning on their unit of choice. As soon as I walked through the double doors and looked around, I knew it. *They thought I was an addict.*

The age of the patients seemed to have dropped by nearly twenty years. They were jittery, wiry, short-tempered, and quick-witted like myself. Worst of all, there was yet another meeting listed after dinner. The schedule said either A.A. or N.A. meetings.

My roommate's name was Thomas. He was a scruffy guy, thirty-five years old, and an opiate addict. He was admitted in the afternoon shortly after I was. We talked for a while, but after dinner he started to feel sick and went to bed. The sound of his vomiting woke me up around five a.m., shortly before vital signs would be checked. Poor Thomas. He must have thrown up at least a dozen times before breakfast. His sickness threw me into a really, really bad mood. I sat down in the common area and looked at the big clock on the wall, feeling guilty for blowing off group therapy on my first full day in Unit 6.

"Zach, either come to group therapy or go to your room!"

I looked up to see who was yelling at me. It was Wade the group therapist, a bear of a man. I'd seen him walking the halls but never thought much of him. Wade just rubbed me the wrong way.

"I'm not going," I replied, storming out of the common area

and slamming my door. Several minutes later my childish mistake led to guilt, which led to sulking. I decided to suck it up and go listen to Wade's group therapy.

"Sick and tired," he kept repeating. "You have to be sick and tired of being sick and tired."

- Six Weeks Later -

Life was in a progressive state. I was working again, paying bills, not smoking weed, and trying to stay away from hard drugs. But, I was still searching for that fix. The Klonopin helped take the edge off for a while, but it just wasn't the feeling I desired.

I overheard someone talking about this stuff legally sold in tobacco shops and corner markets called *spice*. I'd heard about spice over the holidays, though I never paid it much attention. Now, of course, I had to try it. *It's legal, how bad can it be?* My first experience with spice tripped me out, bad. It felt a little bit like a marijuana high, but completely different at the same time. I threw the rest away and said, "Hell no!" Close to a month went by before I tried again. *Maybe I just smoked a bad batch, or a bad brand of spice?*

"Try this kind," a guy said. "It will give you a weed high without all the spins and trippy shit." That guy was right. I thought I'd hit the jackpot; it was legal, there was no need to worry about running out, and I didn't have to smoke pot anymore.

However, gradually my anxiety got worse and worse. It was not an overnight deal, but spice turned me into a monster —

an extremely paranoid, overly terrified monster. The high dose of Klonopin wasn't even touching my anxiety anymore. I went to see my regular doctor, who started me on a low dose of Zyprexa to help with the paranoia. "You're staying away from spice and bath salts, right?" he asked during my visit.

"Yes, of course," was my rushed and shocked response. *How dare he? He needs to stay out of my business and just give me medicines for my symptoms.* Still not thinking that the spice was the cause of my anxiety, I continued to smoke it daily until my breakdown.

It was a Saturday morning.

I was supposed to go into work, but I couldn't. *Why the crying? Why the fear and paranoia?* I texted my boss and told him I just couldn't do it anymore. My text to him was, "This is me telling you I cannot work anymore. I'm so sorry."

I was a depressed, anxious, and addicted to failure. What an embarrassment to my family and friends I had become. Now it was finally clear that my life had fallen apart. Thoughts of hurting myself kept reoccurring and tempting me to give up. Even my parents told me that I couldn't keep doing this anymore. They were getting frustrated that I'd always go back to the hospital when something bad happened. In a way, they were right about that. The hospital had become my worry-free safe zone that I used to escape the truth.

"I'm going back to the hospital," I told them. They didn't respond, or even look worried for that matter. "Alright, well, I'm leaving. Bye." I grabbed my bag and pills and flew out the door.

Wade, that bear of a man, happened to walk by as the wiry lady was checking me in. He shook his head. "Listen," he pointed his finger at me, "cut the crap and listen this time."

My head nodded up and down in agreement, and as he walked away it dropped to my chest in pure shame. The crossroads ahead would be very serious, and I fully felt the weight of it this time. *Who's kidding who? You can't do this anymore. There is nothing left for you to learn from this place.*

Towards the end of the week, I was in a conference with Wade (in his office) and my father (on the phone). I remember my dad telling Wade that he was looking into a rehab facility in Atlanta. It just so happened that Wade was familiar with it. He actually spoke highly of the place to my dad and encouraged me to go get the help that I so desperately needed. When our conference was over, he told me some of his own story. He sat across from me, sucking on sugar-free Lifesavers with one leg crossed over the other.

"I wanted to die," he said. "I wanted to bleed out. You have to be sick and tired of being sick and tired. You know what my moment was?" he asked rhetorically. My head shook slowly from side to side this time. "I was addicted to PCP and couldn't get off. In an alley, I took part of a jagged coke can and cut my arm, hoping to bleed out all the way." He was looking me right in the eyes. I knew that pain. His suffering was my suffering. We were the same.

"Go get help," he said softly, still looking me in the eyes. "Go get help."

I knew there were two options left: Either I could trust my parents and Wade by going to get treatment at this facility, or I could be homeless and continue in my ways until jail or death. Inevitably, my choice was to go to rehab in Atlanta. I was not excited. I was terrified, angry as hell. To make things worse, the night before l left for treatment I was told that they wouldn't allow benzos. *What? No Klonopin?* My denial forced this impossibility out of my thoughts.

Wade was all smiles to me the next morning. He was happy, happy that I'd be getting some *real* help. As a tech took me out of the double doors of Unit 6, I looked over to the office to say goodbye to Wade. He was already one step ahead of me, looking me right in the eyes with a smile that I'll never forget. It was a hopeful smile, almost as if he knew something that I didn't. I smiled back, but it was an unsure grin. Wade gave me a gentle nod to reassure me that this would be a good thing. It would be a *good* thing.

Welcome to Atlanta.

Six

We sat through an initial interview before they admitted me into the young adult unit. Afterwards, I waited outside with a small bag of clothes in one hand and a pillow in the other. My dad told me that he was so proud of me for making the choice to get help. I had no response; I simply stood there and smoked cigarettes.

I just remember being so angry that my parents had given me this type of ultimatum. The extra high dose of Klonopin in my system restrained me from vocally acting on my attitude of frustration, but once again I went into shutdown mode. *Whatever*, I thought. *I just don't care*. A voice calling my name interrupted my thoughts. "Zachary? If you and your dad would like to follow me, I'll take you up to the young adult unit."

I sighed, looked at my dad, grabbed my stuff, and followed the man up to the unit. We walked inside the unlocked unit and a nurse came up to greet us. Miss D was her name and wow, did she brighten up the room. She was friendly to the core and full of smiles. For a few minutes she spoke with my dad and cleared up any medication questions that he had. Then it was time to say goodbye to him. We embraced in a quick hug, and then he left.

A few of the guys came up and introduced themselves to me, before a voice called me over to the receptionist desk. "Hey Zach! I'm Lester." I shook his hand. It seemed to swal-

60

low mine whole. "I need you to come in this room real quick. I have to do a search to make sure you don't have any contraband." I nodded, and then followed him into a small private office. Lester made some small talk with me because he could sense my nervousness. He did a good job, even making me laugh a few times. "Alright, baby, you're cool. Go ahead and wait out in the lobby to meet with your doctor." Lester walked me out of the small office and back into the common room. Then he grabbed my bag and pillow and disappeared into another office behind the receptionist counter. For once I sat comfortably, knowing there was nothing prohibited in my belongings. It was the first time that I had nothing to hide, only clothes in my bag.

I sunk deep into the cozy red chair and waited, contemplating the decisions that led me here. Just as I was starting to think too much, another unfamiliar voice called my name.

"Hey Zach, I'm Doctor Tee. Come on back to my office for a moment. Let's chat." I jumped up and followed him into his office.

Dr. Tee was middle-aged, wore glasses, and just had that look, that smart look where you know he can read you. I hated smart doctors. Well, maybe not hate, but the vulnerability was annoying.

I sat down and waited for him to speak. There was a long, awkward silence, almost like he was thinking, "let me have a nice long look at you." When he finally spoke, he asked a few medication questions but mostly listened to me rant about how bad my anxiety was. As he listened to me, he tilted his head from side to side, which was almost humorous. *Would he really take me off Klonopin?* I asked myself. Eventually we discussed the inevitable. Dr. Tee informed me of the one last Klonopin I would take that night before he would discontinue it. Zip. Nada. No More. My brow began to sweat. *Shit*, I thought. *This is the real deal.*

I left his office to go see where I'd be living. There were nearly twenty guys in the young adult male living area, all of whom were close to my age. I was told that we each had a roommate, and the rooms were right next to each other on a long hallway. As I started to introduce myself around the room, it was clear that each one of the guys had a unique charisma and personality. Yes, they were all addicts like myself, but each individual had his own story on how he came to be sitting in rehab.

Besides asking the guys basic rehab questions, I kept mostly quiet my first night. Just before lights out, our sitter (who was also one of our counselors) pulled out what looked like a huge lunchbox. Inside were many different containers full of medicine. When it was my turn, I took my regular medicine along with my last prescribed Klonopin. Several minutes later the pill started to kick in, leaving me worry-free, calm, and at ease. I was left without any thought on what the next six weeks would bring. Every single second of peace was enjoyed, but eventually my eyes grew heavier and heavier, until total exhaustion. I hopped into my cold, comfortable sheets and instantly passed out.

"6:30! Get up!" A voice yelled into my room. It sounded like a Jamaican man. *Didn't I just go to bed?* I sat up to see who was yelling at me.

"Are you Zach?" the man asked.

"Yeah," I said, falling back into my bed.

"Okay, thirty minutes before we leave for breakfast." I looked over to see if my roommate was still asleep. Of course he was, he'd been here for several weeks and was probably accustomed to this wakeup routine by now. I quickly got dressed and left my room.

Most of the guys were already waiting in the young adult lobby. Some of them were asleep in the cozy red chairs, and others were wide-awake and making coffee. Our nighttime sitter was rounding up the few stragglers who didn't want to get up. He was calling out each one of them by name. "Rich, Michael, get the hell up! Everybody's waiting!"

Finally, the two guys came strolling down the hallway. We left the unit and began the long walk down to the cafeteria, where *all* the units ate every meal; the adolescent unit, the detox unit, the adult unit, and the young adult women's unit were all in the cafeteria. It was a busy and loud arena.

Our sitter handed me a roll of tickets. "Here, you need to give one to a kitchen worker at every meal."

"Thanks," I replied. I looked down at the yellow, raffle style tickets and stood in line. The food was plentiful. There were pancakes, bacon, sausage, eggs, grits, hash browns, biscuits, and much more. I helped myself to a bit of everything, including chocolate milk. Then I sat down with the rest of the guys from my unit at our designated table. A weird feeling hit me while looking around the cafeteria. There was something so familiar about everyone. *Did I know these people?*

After breakfast, the young adult men left as a group to go back to our unit home. By now the different counselors, techs, and doctors were starting to arrive. The young adult women also came over from their apartments to our unit. During the daytime, all the activities, therapy sessions, and meetings were held in the young adult men's area. After dinner, the women would go back to their building for the rest of the night.

I saw Miss D behind the receptionist desk handing out morning medications from the lunch box. I waited in line to take my meds, but then remembered there was going to be *no* Klonopin in my box. *Stop thinking about it, you're going to be fine.* I took my pills and went to the morning meeting.

Lester started the day by leading a meeting with everybody in the young adult program, including all the therapists. Then, we split up into different groups for actual therapy. My group had seven other guys and our therapist, Garrett. I introduced myself, then found a seat in the semi-circle of chairs. The session began with each one of us stating our name, how many days we had been clean, and a word to describe how we were feeling at that moment. It was interesting at first, but the longer the session continued, the more uncomfortable and anxious I became. My heart began to race faster and faster. All of this stuff was new and different from my time in the hospital. *Get out of here*, I thought. *Leave this place.*

I jumped out of my chair and walked out of therapy. Lester and Tori, the woman in charge of the entire young adult program, were standing at the receptionist desk.

"Zach, what's wrong baby?" Lester asked.

"I want to leave…I need to leave."

"What's going on??" Tori said, taking over the conversation. Her tone was threatening.

"I don't think you're hearing me correctly!" I barked. "I

want…to…get…out…of…here!" I started pacing up and down the hallway.

"Zach, calm down," Tori replied, her voice becoming tense.

I flung the door open that led to the smoking patio.

"FUCK!" I yelled as loud as possible. The echo cursed back at me. Once more I yelled it. "FUCK!" Louder. I took a big breath to yell beyond my limits. "FUCK!!" Two men walked outside onto the patio, one of them being Garrett.

"Stay the fuck away!" I yelled at him, putting my fists up.

"You're cool man, you're cool," Garrett said calmly, as I bent over and started to puke. The other man came up behind me and put his hand on my shoulder. "Let it out, Zach," he said.

Garrett asked the man if I was vomiting, while Dr. Tee and Tori stepped outside to see what was going on. "Zach, come to my office with me," Dr. Tee said, calm as ever. I nodded my head, still shaking and crying.

"I can't do this," I told Dr. Tee "Why did you cut me off of the Klonopin? You have no idea how bad my anxiety is!"

Dr. Tee looked distraught. "I'm going to send you down to the detox unit so I can give you Tranxene to help with the withdrawals. I see how anxious you are. You got so anxious that you threw up. Go get a few things from your room and we will take you down there."

"Okay," I mumbled. The other man, who was on the smoking patio with Garrett, walked with me to get some clothes. Then he, along with a few other men, escorted me down to the detox cottage.

After they admitted me, a nurse on the floor approached and said that Dr. Tee had ordered a 2 mg injection of Lorazepam.

Thank God, I thought. She gave me the shot, along with a Tranxene pill. Less than a minute later the rush of sedation flooded over my entire body, taking out every last ounce of fight I had left. I feel asleep. A nurse woke me up a few hours later, and in her hand was a small cup with a pill in it. I quickly downed the pill. Again I fell asleep.

I must have been asleep for at least four hours. It was dark outside and the mood in the unit had changed. Dinner was brought up from the cafeteria, but I didn't have an appetite. I sat in a chair in the common room and watched the other patients. Some patients were arguing, some talking to themselves, and some were doing the exact same thing — nothing. That was the loneliest I've been in my entire life. I was totally and utterly lost, confused, and terrified. There was no hope. There was no love. There was only sick and ugly illness.

When I couldn't take the scene anymore, I went back to my room and cried until I feel asleep. The Tranxene knocked me out and I slept straight through the night. I didn't wake up until a tech walked into my room at ten o'clock to check on me.

I walked out onto the main floor to see what was going on. It appeared to be an absolute repeat of yesterday. The only difference was the shining sun through the massive glass windows. Man, I desperately wanted to go outside and feel the breeze and warmth. I needed that sun on my face, anything but staying in this hellhole another night.

A nurse came and gave me medicine, which included Tranxene, but half the dose as my first two pills. "When is Dr. Tee coming down here?" I asked impatiently

"In the next few hours, just before lunch," she replied.

Good, I thought. His return wouldn't be a moment too soon.

The next two hours were spent rehearsing what to say to Dr. Tee. At this point, I was ready to do just about ANYTHING to get out of here. *Forget the Klonopin. I will bite my tongue and accept not having it anymore,* I whispered repeatedly.

After what felt like forever, Dr. Tee came down to see his patients in the psych and detox units. When it was my turn, he took me into a small office far away from the commotion. He sat down and tilted his head. Another awkward silence, but hell, I didn't care.

"Well, you look a bit better," he chirped.

"I feel *a lot* better, Dr. Tee. I'm sorry about flipping out yesterday. I really don't know what happened. I guess I just freaked out or something, but it will not happen again, just please take me back up to the young adult unit."

"Yeah?" he said. "You were taking a lot of Klonopin and your body *doesn't* like not having it. I need to keep you on Tranxene for a few more days, each time a lower dose. I also need you to start taking Depakote to make sure that you don't have any seizures."

"That's fine, I can do that."

He looked at me again for a moment, just thinking to himself. Then he said, "This isn't going to be easy. It takes hard work and you won't feel well for a while."

"I know, I know…I can do it."

"Alright," he replied, after another long contemplation. "I'll get you back to the young adult program in the next few hours." Undeniable relief rushed over me.

"Thank you…" I breathed out, trying not to smile too much.

"Thank you."

-A Day or Two Later -

When I overheard a counselor telling another counselor, "I don't think Zach will make it; he's going to tire himself out," it really got under my skin. I decided to take control of my temper and attitude to prove them wrong. Maybe I was humiliated, or possibly inspired, but either way I did bite my tongue and gutted through the rest of my treatment.

A day in rehab here consisted of waking up at six-thirty, breakfast, meeting, group therapy, and lunch. After lunch we had another group therapy session, a small break, dinner, A.A. or N.A. meeting, meds, another meeting, and then bed just before midnight. One thing is for certain; we didn't have much time to think. They kept us busy from the time we woke up until the time we went to bed. My medications kept me tired and dull most of the time.

I knew that if I couldn't get high, there had to be something during my day that would come close to helping me calm down and relax — hence junk food. It became my new release. I drank so many cartons of chocolate milk each day that the cafeteria ran out. "Someone been drinking all of 'em!" a kitchen worker told me, when I asked why there were no more. Aside from the cafeteria food, I consumed several thousand calories of junk from morning until lights out. I ate cakes, chips, noodles, fries, sodas, shakes, and anything else loaded with genetically modified ingredients.

Before every meal, I would poke my stomach out as far as

possible and say to the guys, "Pooh hungry…Pooh need honey." I had become a fat tub of lard — a sick and sluggish, fat tub of lard. When I would try to workout or play basketball during break, there was no fight or drive in me, none whatsoever. "Ahhhh, I need a cigarette," was my usual excuse to go back outside and smoke.

I do know that some of the gross eating and sluggishness was because of the new medicines. Out of everyone's pillbox, mine was the largest. I was taking Lexapro, Depakote, Inderal, Clonidine, and Trazodone. The Depakote, Inderal, and Clonidine were all new medications, but even with these pills my anxiety was barely touched. Coming off of the 4+ mg of Klonopin per day was the hardest thing I'd ever gone through in my life. Dr. Tee was just trying to help me out the best he could. The Clonidine was supposed to help take the edge off of my restlessness, and the Inderal was for panic attacks. He knew that I was in hell. It was clear to *everyone* how spastic and anxious I was. But, as Wade once said, "this too shall pass."

Tori had originally told me, "Zach, you've got some kind of mood disorder." Dr. Tee thought so as well. *What? A mood disorder?* I didn't know what to think about that. *Why did they seem so certain?* Some of the counselors told me to read up on bipolar disorders, which I did thoroughly, but there was no new knowledge in the two-page pamphlet. All of the signs and symptoms were broad and extremely vague. However, I decided that things couldn't get much worse; I accepted their diagnosis.

The weeks continued to go by slowly, and as they did, I became more and more comfortable with myself, and expressing my pain. It was so effortless to talk about my issues in group therapy because all of the guys had a similar story to my own. None of us addicts had it all together, but all of us had things in common. We talked about *everything* in group therapy. Friends and family problems, death, sex, addiction, love, God, the earth, pain, suffering, hope, and everything in-between. Garrett could always tell when we were feeding him lies. Even though he grilled each one of us, he always offered hope and restoration before the session was over. No matter what we said in group therapy, judgment was never passed our way. How refreshing! For once in my life, the complete honesty, in itself, was satisfying.

I should probably write about the phone conferences. They happened once a week between Garret, myself, and my parents in Greenville. I suppose the purpose was to try and work out unresolved issues and questions regarding what I would do after leaving rehab. These phone conferences started out rough to say the least. Here was my usual way of reacting when something was said by my parents that I didn't agree with.

"That's bullshit! Are you kidding me? No, I will not do that. You don't even understand. What are you talking about?"

For the first few weeks, this was really all that happened. All my bickering and complaining led me nowhere but wanting to get stoned. Garrett would talk with me after the conference and point out the things I did wrong, but also things I did well. As time went on, I learned how to handle everything in a slightly more mature and adult manner. During my moments of improvement, Garrett would say in the background, "That's good, Zach, good. I like that." His encouragement was nice, but I enjoyed the control more than anything. *Was flipping out all my family knew me for? Was I that predictable?* If I didn't flip out, the conversation actually progressed into new territory — something I'd never experienced.

All these phone conferences helped lead to one thing: sober living. It was highly recommended by the staff to transition into a sober living environment after completing the program. I had no clue what halfway houses were like, but I learned that they were intended for addicts who still need some account-ability before re-entering the real world. More accountability and rules were not what I had in mind after leaving. What did I have in mind? Reservations.

A reservation for alcohol, since I was not an alcoholic.

Garrett had said that a lot of addicts and alcoholics cannot get past a reservation. Narcotics were my drug of choice, therefore I knew that I needed to stop using drugs. Look where they got me. *But what about alcohol?* I never ran to alco-hol for comfort. Couldn't I have a few beers to mellow me out instead of smoking or popping pills? According to Garrett and the other therapists, "No, you can't."

That infuriated me. *How can they possibly tell me that I am an alcoholic?* There was so little room for debate that I gave up arguing after a few days. I stopped talking about it, but that doesn't mean that my reservation was resolved. The idea that I could drink normally buried itself deep in my mind.

Garrett brought up sober living during one of our last phone conferences. My parents were definitely on board, and Garrett recommended a specific halfway house that was supposed to be really nice and relaxing. The house itself was actually a group of apartments in a regular apartment complex. There was one in Atlanta and one in Charlotte. If it had to be done, I wanted to be with the guys that were with me in Atlanta. My parents, however, thought that the one in Charlotte would be better. We agreed to disagree.

My phone interview with the halfway house in Charlotte took place one week before I graduated treatment. On one end of the phone was me, and on the other end was a leader and the ten to twelve addicts in their program. They asked me questions about my recovery plans and where I was in my sobriety.

"Well, I am about seven weeks clean and sober."

Seven long and painful weeks. Seven long weeks of sitting in a chair, feeling like I was falling endlessly through the floor.

"We're a good group of guys here, Zach. We'd be happy to have you come to Charlotte and join our community."

"Okay, I guess I'll see you in a week."

Seven

The winter weather had turned grey as my final day in treatment rapidly approached. When it finally came, my parents made the trip down from Greenville to watch the graduation ceremony. They sat quietly while Lester gave a small speech, praising how far I had come in every aspect of my sobriety. Unfortunately, the one staff member who meant the most to me was not there to send me off; Garrett was sick and unable to work that day. Tori informed me that he had called and said, "Give Zach my best wishes, and tell him how proud I am of his work."

Still, it wasn't what I had planned. Garrett had been the most influential counselor and mentor during my time in treatment. He had seen me at my worst and inspired me to keep growing and pursuing sobriety. He was the guy that kept believing in me and pushed me beyond what I thought was possible. It made me feel disoriented when he wasn't there to send me off on my next chapter of life in Charlotte. It just didn't sit right with me.

I exchanged numbers with a few of my friends after the ceremony ended. It was more difficult to say goodbye than I thought it would be, so I did my best to hold back the tears. Dr. Tee, Lester, Tori, and Miss D all gave me hugs and a few words of wisdom. My mind shut down in the moment. Everything became surreal as time blended together into one giant color of emotion. Before I knew it, the noise and drama was gone, I was riding in the car, and my parents were taking me back to Greenville.

The plan was to spend Christmas with my family and siblings, then leave for Charlotte the following day. Even when Christmas morning came, home did not truly feel like home. The cold weather and grey skies from Atlanta seemed to follow me. Nothing felt normal — everything that once felt like home now felt like a nightmare of unfamiliarity.

- Monday -

My dad drove me up to Charlotte in the morning. We didn't talk much during the drive, which was fine with me; I was exhausted. The weather was quite nasty, but as we got closer to Charlotte the grey skies faded into a crystal clear day. It was still cold, but once the sun started shining my mood began to rise. I expected these sober-living apartments to be quite old and ragged, but my thoughts changed once the directions said we were a mile away. The apartments were actually easy on the eyes. It was a fairly nice area and the skyline view of downtown was enticing.

Drew, the leader I spoke with on the phone, was waiting outside for us on the curb. He was about twenty-five years old and thin as a rail. He was dressed real artsy. He was wearing some aviator style glasses and smoking a cigarette like it was going out of style. He motioned for us to park near him.

"You must be Zach! Hi, I'm Drew."

His positivity startled me. I shook his hand quickly while simultaneously saying goodbye to Pops.

"What can I help you grab?" he asked.

"Uh...well, you can get this bag of food. I just have one other bag and a pillow."

He grabbed it like it was an order. "So, I'll take you to your apartment," he said. "Right now, Allen and Ben are the only two guys in there. We're going to stick you in the room with Allen." His speech was quick, but kind. I followed behind him until he stopped at the apartment door and spastically for his keys. Eventually, he found the right key and we walked into a first floor apartment. It was clean and cozy. It smelled fresh and looked like it had been built yesterday.

"That's your room back there," he said, pointing down the hall. "Let's sit down real quick and go over the basic rules and paperwork." I nodded and sat at the table with several documents on it. "It's really not that bad here, Zach," Drew said softly. "We require you to attend six A.A or N.A. meetings a week, have at least a part-time job, and be in your apartment by curfew. That's basically all we ask, but staying sober is the number one priority and we will drug test you every two or three days."

He continued to inform me on the other details as I finished signing the papers and agreement forms. Drew was right, it didn't appear to be as bad as I thought.

"Oh, and we meet once a week on Monday nights at seven. It's like an accountability and big book study. You can meet the guys tonight."

"Sounds good," I said. "What do you want me to do until then?"

"Oh, just chill and get settled in. Your patio is right outside that door, if you smoke."

"Good," I breathed out, relieved that I could still have my nicotine.

"Alright, well you have my number. Call me if you need anything at all. I'll be around." He smiled, put his shades back on, and left. There was a moment of complete silence before I let out a chuckle. *Why was I so worried? This isn't so bad.*

I went to my room to unpack my things and make my bed. When I worked my way into the bathroom, I lined up my five medicine bottles from biggest to smallest on the counter. *My roommate is going to think I'm nuts.* I shook my head and took the pill bottles off the counter and put them back into my toiletry bag.

Once the unpacking was done, I was left with absolutely nothing to do. The complete silence had become awkward and was starting to make me feel alone. I went out on the smoking patio and listened to the traffic for a while, in an attempt to distract myself. The sound of the cars was soothing. People were living their lives on just another normal day. It was just another, normal day.

Several cigarettes later, the sound of traffic zipping by stopped working. That painful feeling started pushing its way back into my head. But, before I allowed myself to be completely consumed with fear, I jumped up and went back inside.

Someone's keys were jingling outside my apartment door. I froze in the middle of the living room. The door flung open.

"Oh… hi, I'm Ben. You must be the new guy."

"Yeah, I'm Zach." I walked over and routinely shook his hand.

"Is Allen here?" he asked.

"No, it's just been me here for the last few hours."

"Ah, gotcha," he said.

Ben, who was wearing a barista uniform, started unloading several bags of leftover pastries. I immediately took advantage of his presence and started firing off questions.

I asked about the guys in the program, the rules, and the apartment complex itself — mainly the gym. He was very helpful with his answers, but I noticed that he never extended the conversation to ask anything about me. Nothing at all.

"So, are you riding with me to the group meeting?" Ben asked. "It's like five minutes down the road at this little church."

"That would be nice," I replied.

"Okay, I'll let you know when it's time to go."

That was the end of our conversation. I was confused at Ben's hostility, so I went back to my room and isolated until it was time to leave for the group meeting.

There were already several guys in the program smoking and chatting when we pulled up. I was relieved to see that Drew was already there and, of course, he looked chill and worry-free. When he finally noticed me standing there, he motioned me to come over his way.

"Zach, meet the guys." I swallowed the lump in my throat and began introducing myself. "Zach just got here today from South Carolina." I nodded my head and smiled, but secretly I was hoping that the meeting would begin soon. My face was starting to turn red and my voice was shaky.

"Alright guys, let's head inside and get started," Drew announced through the noise. *Whew.*

One by one, we put out our cigarettes and walked inside to a small meeting room in the church. The old wooden table we sat at was entirely too large; there were only a dozen or so of us in the program. We looked like the knights of the Round Table with the amount of space in-between us. I sat down in a chair right next to Drew.

"Did you bring your big book?" he whispered to me.

"Oh no, I forgot man. I'm sorry."

"No no, don't worry about it. Here, use mine tonight." He handed me an old, worn-in A.A. book. It was beautiful, full of character and time. Then, just as he was about to start the meeting, the door flew open.

"Damn, Allen. It's about time!" someone hollered sarcastically.

I looked over to see Drew's reaction. He just sighed, "Come on Allen, we're trying to get this thing started." Allen rushed over to an empty seat at the table.

Drew restarted the meeting by having each one of us give an update on our sobriety, our jobs, and any issues we needed to discuss with the group. I listened carefully to get a better feel for the guys I'd be spending time with. Allen went last and gave an incredibly insecure, but honest update. He must have talked for at least fifteen minutes, but everyone gave him their attention, along with encouraging words and perspective once he was finished.

When the meeting concluded, I rode back to the apartment with Ben, not Allen. I didn't want things to be anymore stressful than they already were. When we walked inside, Allen was folding laundry in our shared bedroom. I walked in to introduce myself.

"Hey, I'm Zach." I reached out to shake his hand.

"Allen, nice to meet you," he replied.

It was easy to tell that I would get along much better with Allen than Ben. In fact, we jumped into a conversation that lasted several hours after this brief introduction. It was like we were on the exact same page, not only in our sobriety, but life in general. I found out that he dealt with a lot of social anxiety like myself. We were both confused and scared, and neither of us really knew who we were yet. His empathy on my first day in Charlotte was a comfort.

- Tuesday -

I stayed inside for almost the entire day, searching the Internet to see what jobs were available. Allen and Ben were at work, which left the apartment completely silent. I didn't have a car to go anywhere, and I was way too scared to venture off by myself on a bus. Where would I go? How would I get back? Who do I talk to? This sense of being stuck combined with not knowing anyone made me even more helpless. I was actually happy when Ben got back from work around five o'clock. He looked stressed when he walked in, but I couldn't keep my mouth shut.

"Hey, what's up, Ben? How did work go?" I asked a little too eagerly.

"Um, it was good," he mumbled. He had several bags from work that he was unloading on the kitchen counter.

"What did you bring home today, anything good?"

"Just leftovers," he replied, still not looking at me.

"Nice."

I started to walk away after sensing his get-away-from-me vibe, but Ben hollered across the room. "Have you hit a meeting yet today?"

I spun around, "No, actually I haven't."

"Well, I'm going to get something to eat and then go to my home group. The meeting is at seven. You can come to that one with me."

I nodded, "Is it an A.A. or N.A. meeting?"

"A.A meeting," he said impatiently. "So, are you going to come?"

"Well, I don't know where else I'd hit a meeting. What time do we have to leave?"

He thought for a moment. "Let's leave at 6:30. I want to talk to some people before it starts."

More new people, I thought. *Exactly what I had in mind.*

"That sounds good," I said, trying to be positive. "I'll be ready at 6:30."

It was cold, wet, and rainy when we arrived at the meeting location, again at a church. Ben left my side almost instantly to talk with some people he knew. He introduced me but they didn't seem appealing, so I walked off to smoke a cigarette. Eventually, he found me again and we walked inside to get a seat.

Throughout the entire meeting I kept thinking how weird these A.A. meetings were. *What were they even talking about?* Steps, sponsors, was this a cult? I'd been to a lot of A.A.

meetings during treatment in Atlanta, but there were a lot of younger addicts involved. The people at this meeting were all older. Ben and I were the youngest people there, and I couldn't have cared less about what these old folks had to say; they were not the happiest of alcoholics, but maybe that's because they were sober. Where was their excitement? Where was their hope? I looked down at the watch on my hand. It was moving slowly, and the more I stared at it the longer the meeting seemed to last.

The meeting finally came to a close after an hour. Ben went to talk to his friends again, so I decided to walk away again, acting like there was an important phone call. It worked. Twenty minutes later I heard him call my name. "Zach, you ready to go?" he called out.

"Yes, I am ready." *Good Lord, it's about time.*

He said goodbye to his friends, then we ran through the heavy rain to his car. I didn't speak much on the way back; the sound of the rain hitting the windshield made my eyes want to close. I was also hungry, angry, lonely, and tired. Everything about this Tuesday had been depressing — everything.

Allen was in the living room watching TV when we got back. Ben went straight to his room, but I stayed in the kitchen to get some food.

"How was your meeting?" Allen asked.

I laughed. "How'd you know we were at a meeting?"

"Ben brought his big book inside," He said, pointing to the blue book on the counter.

"Well, it was alright, but there was hardly anyone our age." I looked to see if Ben was tucked away in his room before saying, "Dude, what are those A.A. people talking about? I don't get this stuff."

Allen laughed. "Why don't you roll with me to a different meeting tomorrow. My home group has a bunch of people in their twenties. You just have to find that right group, you know?"

I sighed, "No, not really, but I'll check out your home group. It can't be worse than the meeting Ben took me to tonight."

- Wednesday -

It would be nice to say that Wednesday was a lot better than Tuesday, but it wasn't. It felt like Groundhog Day, minus the social interaction. I ventured off to the gym when a wave of bravery hit me, but my workout was pitiful and lacked any intensity. I threw in the towel after twenty minutes and began the long walk back to the apartment.

It was a harsh reality.

I wanted to go anywhere, anywhere but back to that place alone, fearful, and depressed. But, at the same time, there was nowhere else that I'd rather go than back to that dark place.

Why couldn't I face the world? What was holding me back and causing me to be so terrified of everything?

My phone started vibrating in my sweatpants. "Hello… "

"Zach! Hey man, what's going on?" It was Drew to the rescue.

"Not much. I'm walking back from the gym," I huffed through the phone.

"Oh, nice. I'm just calling to check in with you. I wanted to make sure you are doing okay."

I nearly broke down in tears. "I'm doing okay. Got an appointment with a new doctor tomorrow, which is good…I guess."

"That *is* good! Do you need a ride?" he said without hesitation.

"No, actually my mom is driving up from Greenville. She set up the appointment and wants to meet him or whatever."

"Oh, okay," he replied. There was a brief silence. "Hey, if you do ever need a ride anywhere or want help on your job hunt, feel free to ask. That's what I'm here for."

I was really holding back the tears now. "Thanks Drew, I'll let you know."

"Please do," he said. "Which meeting are you hitting tonight?"

"Well, Allen invited me to his home group, so I'm gonna check that out. He said it's a bit of a younger crowd, which would be nice."

"Yeah, that is a good group," he said, "I've been there many times. Let me know what you think. Call me later if you need anything."

"Thanks Drew, I will. Thanks for calling." I hung up the phone.

- Thursday -

The alarm clock put me in a frenzy when it went off at nine. I looked out the window to see what the weather was like. *Thank God,* it wasn't raining. Mom had already left Greenville to pick me up for our appointment with this new doctor, so I hurried to get ready. I prayed several times and asked God to let this new doctor give me something, anything, to help with this depression, worry, and anxiety. It was eating me alive. This voice in my head kept telling me how pathetic I was. *Another doctor? Really? What's this, like number six this year?*

I was tired of these doctors looking into my eyes and trying to find the problem. It was humiliating and demeaning. I didn't want to have yet another doctor analyze me, diagnose me, and give me a different pill. Although, if that pill would help me calm down and relax, I would probably be interested. This appointment, I thought, would be more paperwork, different pills, and no promise of results.

My bickering must have come as a shock to my mom, as I complained the entire way to his office. "What's this guy's name?" I asked impatiently.

"Lord, Dr. Lord." She responded quietly.

"Do I really have to talk about EVERYTHING again? It's getting exhausting." She didn't say anything. She just kept driving with a half-smile, like she was holding back a justifiable response.

We pulled up to the building and hurried inside. As expected, there were several pages of patient information forms that had to be filled out before I could see this Lord doctor.

"Here," I said to my mom, "Will you fill out this insurance stuff please?"

She patiently reached for the clipboard and started filling out the adult section. This was good because it gave me enough time to figure out how I was going to tell this doctor about the years and years of whatever it was that I suffered from, or what was wrong with me.

When it was my turn to be seen, Dr. Lord walked down the stairs of this house-like office and called my name. He gave me an overly firm handshake and asked for me to join him in his office. My mom grabbed her purse expecting to come with us, but Dr. Lord asked if she would stay downstairs for the first half of the appointment. She nodded her head, he smiled, and I followed him up the doll-size staircase to his office.

"So, Zachary, how are you doing today?"

"I'm anxious," I replied, sitting down in a firm, leathery chair.

He proceeded to ask a few questions about what I was doing, where I was living, and why I was here to see him. I fired off answers quickly and quietly.

He nodded behind his rectangular framed glasses. "Well, I'd like it if you could tell me about your drug use. When did it start, what did you use, things like that…"

I nearly fell out of the chair when he asked me this. My mind almost went blank from not knowing where or how to start my timeline. A huge sigh slipped out of my mouth and I took in a big breath. Then I blurted out as much information as my brain would allow. It was like watching that car accident you saw coming. When I finished, his head was still down in the notepad and his hands were writing away information. The dead silence reflected back the words I had just spewed. They were ugly and detestable. It almost made me sick hearing my own thoughts.

"Now, what medications are you currently taking?" he asked with his face still behind the paper. The question made me cringe. It was another blow to my already pathetic and weakened ego.

"Lexapro in the morning, Inderal twice a day, Clonidine twice a day, Depakote twice a day, and Zyprexa at bedtime."

I was expecting a facial reaction from him, but he just kept on taking notes. He hadn't made eye contact with me since I began talking, but that didn't bother me; it helped me stop sweating so much.

"Alright Zach, wait here while I go get your mom."

He closed the notebook and left the office. I took a deep breath and tried not to think. Less than a minute later he returned with my mom, who then sat down in a chair next to me. Dr. Lord was sitting at his desk across from us with one leg crossed over the other and his hands folded together below his chin. We waited patiently for him to speak.

"Zachary, I'm going to be honest with you. I don't see anything that points to you being bi-polar, or even having a mood disorder. I think you may have a little anxiety, but eventually I think you should be able to stop most of this medication, if not all of it."

I sat there silently, absolutely stupefied by what I had just heard. He continued with directions before I even had a chance to respond. "I'd like for you to take half of the dose of Zyprexa for one week, then stop. You're on a low dose so it shouldn't be a problem. We'll start with that and I'll see you in one week."

I panicked.

"I really need something for this anxiety." I said, begging at this point. "I can't take this for too much longer,"

What an incredibly long five seconds. His exact response I cannot remember, but it was something along the lines of "No."

All hope of getting some relief from this hell vanished, and a deep hatred for the man took hope's place. I stood up. "Fuck you!" I said, looking him in the eye, and then rushing out of his office. My whole body was vibrating with rage. It took me several attempts before successfully lighting up a cigarette.

For the next fifteen minutes I paced back and forth in the beautiful weather, weighing my options and debating my next move. My mom stepped outside the office and walked over to the car. When she unlocked the doors, I quickly stepped in and fastened my seatbelt. "Let's get out of here," I said, gritting my teeth. "That guy's an idiot." Disappointment and sadness washed over her face as she started the engine and pulled out of the parking lot.

"Dr. Lord said you're just angry because he didn't give you what you wanted."

I froze. "Stop the car," I said robotically. "Pull the car over."

Eventually, she was able to pull over off of the main road and onto a side street. As soon as she did, I jumped out, slammed the door shut, and leaned up against the side with my arms crossed. Looking off into the distance, a part of me gave up the fight and surrendered to my anxiety. *Was Dr. Lord right in saying that?* I asked myself. It's true, I *was* angry because he didn't give me what I wanted. But, what I wanted most was to be free.

Eight

New Year's Eve fell on a Saturday night. A group of us guys in the program had planned on going out to welcome in 2012. There was Allen, Ben, Kurt, and myself. How we landed in a saloon style venue I have no idea, but at eleven p.m. we went out to enjoy a sober celebration. Technically we broke curfew, but Drew was lenient on that issue and we weren't worried about getting into trouble. This saloon was a massive place. It appeared that everyone in Charlotte, or at least the country folk, had come out to celebrate. There were two-dollar beers, dollar shots, some drugs, and all types of partying going on from the second we walked in.

My blood started flowing and my head began to bob to the music. "Yo, Allen!" I yelled. "Let's go out back and smoke a cigarette." He nodded as we tried to navigate to the outside smoking section of the club. We left Kurt and Ben, who were already dancing away with some girls. They didn't even notice us leaving.

"Dude," said Allen, "This place is where it's at tonight!" At least, I think that's what he said. I could barely hear him through the yelling and drunken laughs. We stepped outside to the slam-packed smoking section that was engulfed in a giant cloud of smoke. I huffed down several cigarettes as my hands were shaking with excitement. "Alright, I can't even move. Let's go back inside," I yelled to Allen. He followed me through the maze of smoke and people until we got back inside the club.

We spent a few minutes watching some drunks push the mechanical bull to its limit. Each person fell off within seconds from being so hammered. "I want a beer man," I said to Allen while laughing. It was partially a joke, but I really just wanted to hear him say, "I want one too."

He did. He said it, but then he took my half-joke one step further and looked over to see if Kurt and Ben were still dancing. I looked too, but the place was just so crowded that it was really impossible to locate them. Allen didn't say anything as he pointed to an employee with a cooler who was handing out two-dollar beers. I followed him sheepishly over to the counter. He looked at me, I looked at him. He shrugged his shoulders, I shrugged my shoulders. He bought a beer, then I bought a beer. Before I even took the time to weigh this decision, the beer was down the hatch. Gone. The tingling hit my head and *wow* did it feel good. I cursed sobriety and the program. "Let's go over to the main floor!" I yelled to Allen. "The ball drops in ten minutes!"

We quickly threw away our empty bottles and went onto the main dance floor. The band was killing it on stage, making me want to get a thousand more beers and let myself go. But, then it hit me, and my stomach dropped. I had just relapsed. 58 days of hell and overcoming impossible odds went down the hatch. *You blew it man. You will get kicked out of recovery. You just flipped your parents the bird, who fought, kicked, cried, and prayed desperately for you to get sober. You ruined it…over one beer.*

My jaw clamped down, teeth clenched as I pushed the panic deep down into my gut. *No, not now. Don't get caught up now, panic later.* The crowd was getting louder. More and more people were packing onto the dance floor.

The band was about to start the countdown.

"Ten…nine…eight…" The crowd got louder and louder. "Seven…six…five…four…" Louder and louder, "Three…two…one…HAPPY NEW YEAR!"

It became so loud that all I heard was silence. I looked around at the people who were jumping and dancing and hugging and kissing. *What have I done.* When the crowd eventually thinned out, we noticed that Kurt and Ben had spotted us and were walking our way.

"Where did you guys run off to?" Kurt asked. "We've been looking for ya'll for like an hour!"

Allen opened his mouth before I had a chance to lie. "We went outside to smoke and then you guys just disappeared." He did sound convincing, but maybe that's because he was telling at least half of the truth.

"Either way," replied Ben, "We have to leave. It's getting late."

We all agreed, and the four of us started the long hike through the field to where we had parked. On the way out, Kurt kept bragging about the girls he and Ben were dancing with. "Yeah man, they loved me…got one girl's number too!" Ben laughed at Kurt's rampant exaggeration, while Allen just shook his head. It seemed like they weren't suspicious about anything, and that eased my mind about not getting caught. Still, the honesty that I'd grown to love and be proud of was gone, and now I would have to revert back to being a liar.

Fortunately, Drew was not tapping his foot waiting on us when we pulled up to the apartment at 1 o'clock. *What a relief.*

Kurt said goodnight and went upstairs to his apartment.

"Alright, I'm hitting the sack," Ben said. "Goodnight." He went into his room and shut the door. I motioned for Allen to follow me into our room, just in case Ben could hear us over the tv.

I shut the door. "Dude," I said, putting my hands up to my face. "This cannot leave us. Promise me man, I can't afford to get kicked out."

"I can't either! I'm not going to tell anyone," he said, almost whispering.

I felt my stomach start to calm down. "Okay, good, just needed to make sure this stays between the two of us."

With that taken care of, we both went to bed. My thoughts raced as usual, but I blocked out the hurt and fear of my secret being exposed. *You're angry,* I told myself. *It's not your fault.* Turning my fear into anger made me feel better about the situation because it really *wasn't* my fault. It was Dr. Lord's fault, my parent's fault, but not mine. Pain was not an option. At least I could live with myself being angry.

- The Next Monday -

I followed Dr. Lord's directions and came off of the Zyprexa within a week. The only reason I did was because it was one less medication to constantly worry about taking every day. Keeping track of my medications was a job in itself. My schedule was: wake up and take my Lexapro, Clonidine, Inderal. In the afternoon it was Inderal and Clonidine, and then Depakote at night.

Allen and I continued to grow as friends, and soon we were inseparable. Our heavy secret was the glue of the friendship. Most nights we would hit a meeting, and then afterwards we'd go to downtown Charlotte for something fun to do. Neither of us drank at these clubs because that would mean we had relapsed, *and we hadn't*. We pushed the secret away until neither of us even acknowledged that it happened.

One night after a meeting, Allen said he wanted to stop by a coffee shop and say hello to some of his old friends. "Sure man," was my response. I had a gut feeling that the friends he was referring to were some of his old using buddies, but I didn't care enough to bring it up.

We sat outside of the coffee shop in this secluded, fenced in area. It was dark; the street lamps were the only light that shined on us. Allen's friends looked like some hippies, which is why I wasn't surprised when the girl pulled out a bowl, packed some weed in it, and fired it up. They passed it around between themselves, while Ben and I sat there drooling and smoking cigarettes. The smell was intoxicating. It had been over two months since I had smoked. Consequently, I had forgotten the luring smell of really good weed. *Really good weed.* It was too inviting.

"Hey, can I get a small hit of that?" I asked the girl.

"Hell yeah, this is some good shit," she replied. I looked at Allen to make sure he didn't have a judgmental look on his face. Nope, he didn't, just a half-smirk while he shrugged his shoulders, almost encouraging me to see what would happen. I took a hit of the bowl, and then a few more. It was everything I missed.

I sat back and took a deep breath. The high started to creep up my skull, becoming more intense with each minute that passed. I looked around at Allen and his friends. Then, the paranoia hit me like it never had before. *Was this weed laced? I'm super high right now. Is Allen trying to set me up?* I could feel my heart beating out of my chest, my insides getting colder and my throat disappearing.

I was able to get Allen's attention once his friends turned the conversation amongst themselves. "Dude, I gotta go," I whispered, my eyes barely open. Allen could tell that I was freaking out, so he played it cool and told them we had to leave. I nodded goodbye to them and rushed to get into Allen's car.

"I'm so high man. Please tell me you have some eye drops before I have to go into the apartment."

It's like he was one step ahead of me. He reached into his driver door and pulled out some eye drops. "Are you alright dude?" he asked. " Do you want to drive around for a little bit before we go home?"

"Yes, actually I do," I blurted out. "I can't go back looking like this. Ben will know I'm high."

He looked over at me. "Yeah, you do look really high. No worries man, we will go get some food or something."

We spent the next hour driving around and picking up food. I also made sure to smoke several cigarettes before going back to our apartment. When we pulled up, I took a quick look in the mirror to make sure my eyes were purely white before walking in. We opened the door to find Ben in the living room watching a show with John, another guy in our program. I must have been super paranoid. They didn't do or say anything out of the ordinary. *Why did I assume they knew what was going on in my head?* Regardless, I rushed back to my room, shut my door, and started to watch a movie. I could hear Allen, Ben, and John laughing and having a good time in the other room, so I knew that it was my own paranoia that had gotten the best of me. Still, there was no way Ben could find out; he would be sure to rat on me.

I was almost asleep, but I jolted out of bed when I remembered.

Drug testing was the next morning.

I grabbed a cup and started chugging water, drink after drink after drink until I couldn't drink anymore without wanting to throw up. Then I set my alarm clock to go off an hour before the drug-testing guy would come. As soon as the alarm went off in the morning, I drank and drank and drank again, until my urine was as clear as could be. I waited for the knock, which was right on time. The drug-testing guy came in with his medical bag and cups. I could barely hold my bladder, so I asked to go first. My excuse was being "tired." The thought occurred to me afterwards that my plan might not work. I might get caught, but then again, there are always false positives and I could blame it on that.

Three days later, I still had not received a call from Drew regarding my drug test. It worked. My plan had succeeded, but unfortunately I couldn't keep a secret.

I don't remember why, but I did tell Ben a few days later about the beer I'd drank during our New Year's Eve celebration at the saloon. I suppose I was feeling safe or invincible. *But why couldn't I have kept my mouth shut?* Ben said that I messed up, but he wouldn't say anything to Drew. Mistake, big mistake. It was bound to happen.

Ben and I got into a predominately verbal fight a week later over who knows what, during which he said he had exposed Allen and myself. In a moment of pure rage, I pushed him into a wall and began to scream in his face. He pushed me away and we took turns saying the most hurtful and provocative things we could possibly think of. John got involved too, also saying that it was my fault. "Fuck you too, John!" I yelled, before storming out of the apartment.

It just so happened that Drew and Chris, the other leader of the program, were outside of the apartment. I haven't mentioned Chris previously because he was rarely around. He asked me what was going on, while Drew went inside the apartment to talk with Ben and John. I explained to him that I got into a fight with Ben, but he knew the truth.

"We all know about what happened at the club on New Year's Eve," He said. "We're actually here because of it. There's going to be a meeting with the whole community once things settle down."

I felt my lungs inhale a full, deep breath, and then let it out with a sigh of relief. The truth had been exposed and it was a relief, a big relief, even if they kicked me out.

"So, what's going to happen?" I asked Chris. "Are Allen and I getting kicked out?"

He paused, before answering my question of fate. "Truthfully, I don't know. Drew and I report to the manager of the program, Stacy. You guys never see her, but you will in thirty minutes. She is going to have the final say." I had never met Stacy, but Tori in Atlanta told me that she was friends with her, and that meant only one thing: she didn't play games.

Chris sent me to another apartment in our unit where several of the guys had already gathered to await the spontaneous meeting. Most of them didn't know what was going on, but Kurt and Allen were sitting on a couch clearly aware that we were in some big trouble. The rest of the guys walked in and sat down, including Ben and John. I could barely look at them without wanting to jump up and knock both of them out cold. Last, but not least, Stacy, Chris, and Drew walked into the apartment, and the room instantly became silent. Stacy began the dialogue while Drew and Chris sat with their heads down, as if they too were about to be grilled.

"So," Stacy said, "I heard that a couple of you guys went out on New Year's Eve to a bar or club. Who all went?" She looked around the room as Kurt, Ben, Allen and myself each raised our hand. "What made you guys think that was okay, or a smart thing to do?"

Kurt spoke up. "We planned on just staying for a few minutes. None of us wanted to party or anything."

"Were you guys together the entire time?" Stacy asked Kurt, the only one willing to give an explanation at the moment.

"No," he replied. "We got separated after a while. It was only Ben and I for the rest of the time, I can't answer for Zach or Allen."

Stacy turned to Ben, "Did you or Kurt drink?"

"No, ma'am!" Kurt said.

"I wasn't talking to you," Stacy said. She turned to Ben and asked him the question one more time.

"No, we didn't drink," he said softly.

I figured it was now time for Stacy to ask Allen and I some questions, which she did. She looked over at Allen. "Did you drink anything, Allen?"

"Yes, I had one beer," he replied. The room got very quiet, with little to no eye contact with one another.

"Did you drink, Zach?" she asked.

"Yes, I also had one beer," I replied, looking her right in the eye. I didn't want to, but I felt like that would be my best option for getting a second chance.

I continued to speak the truth, "I also took a few hits off a bowl the other night, but that's it."

"Did any of you guys know about this?" she asked Kurt and Ben. "No Ma'am," Kurt said. "I didn't have a clue that this happened."

Then Ben spoke up, "Zach told me a few days ago that he and Allen had a beer at the club, but that's all I knew."

Stacy went on to ask about what had happened recently between Ben and myself. I started with my own version of the story, but Ben interrupted soon after, which then turned into a shouting match.

"Alright, enough!" Stacy yelled. I felt my blood pressure rising up again. "Zach, you need to apologize to Ben and John."

If I had not been in this room with everyone, I would have cursed them again. But instead, I found myself apologizing, first to John, and then to Ben.

"Alright, thank you," she said. "Now, Ben, you need to apologize to Zach."

"No," replied Ben, "I'm not giving him an apology."

"Dude, you called me a faggot!" I yelled at Ben. "Apologize!"

The room became really quiet again, but John ended the silence by saying, "Aw come on, Ben. Just apologize so we can move on from this shit." I waited, we all waited to see what would happen.

"No," said Ben. John, Kurt, and Allen all let out a sigh that expressed their own frustrations with Ben. My anger was boiling over. I was vibrating with rage.

"Fine!" I yelled at Ben. "That's bullshit! I'm leaving."

I stood up from the couch and walked outside before bursting into tears from the anger. I called my mom and told her what was going on and that I was getting kicked out. There was no doubt that she was upset on the phone, but to my surprise she said she would come pick me up. I immediately went back to my room and started to pack my things. Drew came into the apartment as I was getting my things out of the bathroom.

"I'm so sorry, Zach," he said, shaking his head. "That shouldn't have happened. Ben really should have apologized to you." He was visibly upset. I almost felt bad for him, but instead of showing signs of guilt I chose to play the victim card.

"It's not your fault. It's just not going to work out," I said.

Drew let out an overly long sigh. "This really shouldn't have gotten out of hand. It's partially my fault and I'm really sorry about that. What can I help you get?" he asked softly.

"You can grab my computer," I mumbled. "I got the rest."

He snatched my computer like it was an order and followed me outside to a grassy area. There we sat on the curb, smoking cigarettes and waiting. We didn't talk much, and I'm sure it's because we were both replaying the previous events in our heads. The sun was starting to set and the sky was brushed with bright colors of red and orange.

I saw my mom pull up with sunglasses on and a tense look on her face. She stayed in the car and kept it running while I threw my stuff into the back seats. I shook Drew's hand, said thank you, and climbed inside. He motioned for me to roll down the window.

"Let me know if I can do anything for you, okay? Once again, I'm really sorry about this."

"Thanks, I will," I replied while buckling my seatbelt.

Mom began to drive off. I looked in the mirror and watched Drew finish his cigarette and stomp it out on the ground again, like he did when I first met him.

Just like that, my chapter of life in Charlotte was done.

Drew was one of the only people whose sobriety I actually envied. It was easy to tell how comfortable and content he was living a lifestyle free of drugs and alcohol. One day, I hope to thank him.

Nine

We didn't speak much on the way back to Greenville, although I did ask her the usual question, "Are you and Pop going to let me stay with you?" Her answer was not good. She replied with, "I don't know what we're going to do."

Mentally, I prepared myself for anything.

We pulled into the driveway and my mom went inside. I took a minute to relive all the events that seemed to happen so fast. Just eight hours ago, I was sitting in the apartment without a clue that my secret had already been exposed, or that I'd be leaving. The following afternoon my dad had a serious talk with me. He wrote up a list of conditions that I *must* abide by to live in their house. This time it was clear that he was not going to be hesitant at all to kick me to the curb if I started to use again.

"Get a job, go to meetings, pay your bills, be kind to everyone, meet with a counselor once a week, see your doctor," were key things on his list of rules.

I did have lot of guilt from the things I put them through, and the grace that my dad was giving me made me feel even worse. I almost wanted them to be done with me so I didn't have to live with such guilt. But since they were giving me another chance, I would try my best to behave. It fueled me to find employment and see a counselor who could help with the anxiety.

Before starting my job search, my parents thought it would

help to meet with a therapist that could give me tips on over-coming anxiety without benzos. That was my first priority. Priority number two would be advice on what to do next and how to do it.

My therapist's name was Larry. He was a very laid back guy, but he was well-versed in giving real world advice. His calm demeanor relaxed me, and in some ways, it's what me coming back to see him. We met once a week, and at the beginning of each session he would break the ice with small talk about sports, current news, or anything that might open up lanes for the serious talk. When the time was right, we would talk about anxiety — more specifically, how to train my brain to ac-knowledge the unrealistic nature of fear or phobias. Larry always had great insight on realistic vs. unrealistic thinking. The more issues I was willing to discuss, the better I felt in the following weeks. However, there was one topic that I would always revert to.

"How do I get through an interview without freaking out? How can I go out into large groups of people without all these physically embarrassing symptoms?"

Larry's answer was that a lot of people have social anxiety. "It's not that uncommon. Everyone gets nervous for a job interview, that's natural." His answer made a lot of sense, so I wondered how all of these irrational thoughts had escaped my radar for the past four years. Even though I was beginning to acknowledge my irrational thinking, it wasn't enough for me to take a real chance. My job search started off very slowly because of this.

I started by looking online for jobs. Then I met with Larry to tell him of my progress and ask for advice on my next step.

One of his assignments was to go and introduce myself to employers, especially the places I had already applied at online. He told me to smile, shake some hands, and causally ask about employment. What I loved most about Larry was his acknowledgment and praise for even the simplest progress, no matter how juvenile or small it seemed. The tiniest steps of progress that most people would disregard were labeled as heroic. I wasn't lazy. I loved working and making money. It was getting the job that was the hard part — the part I feared the most. I knew that if I could just get over that hump, I would do just fine on the laboring side.

As the next few weeks went by, I followed Larry's advice and introduced myself to some managers. I always took my Inderal before going out on my job search; it helped keep my embarrassing physical symptoms to a minimum, like sweaty and clammy hands.

Within a few weeks I had landed a job. It was a restaurant job, very simple with no real responsibility other than making the customers happy. It was perfect for getting back into the swing of things. The people were great, the hours were good, and I was content with the pay. For the next several months, I was able to get back out into society on a regular basis via my job. The night shifts were my favorite because they allowed me to skip the A.A meetings that I was supposed to be going to.

I managed life for a while, but that voice in my head was persistent; the voice that told me I could drink after work or occasionally smoke some pot to relax and ease my stress. It was not an overnight change, but once it began it was nearly impossible to stop. I found myself drinking most nights after work at the bowling ally bar. I liked that it was a quiet place, free from drama and a lot of people. It was cozy and the muffled sound of pins getting knocked over was therapeutic. I would stay at the bar for about an hour, and on my way home I'd pick up some beer at the store.

There were hardly, if any, consequences for quite some time. If my family had known some of these things it would have been a different story. But, after a solid two months, I thought that I had moved on from my dangerously addictive tendencies. There was a girl at work, too. She was really cute and kind with a great personality. She didn't see a problem with occasionally smoking weed, which was also a plus. Once we started dating, our relationship went from zero to a hundred within weeks. All of my insecurities were forced on this girl. I desperately needed her, depended on her, and craved her love and attention. I'd completely forgotten about my sobriety or that I had attended rehab quite recently, going through some of the worst withdrawals and terror of my entire life. My using, combined with this girl, made for a nasty disaster. It was then that the negative consequences started to take place.

Before going out for drinks one night, I took several painkillers and a few benzos I'd been able to snag from an old using buddy. I spent the rest of that night drinking like a fish. The next morning I was hung over and sick as a dog, clearly not capable of going in to work. I called my boss and left a voicemail saying that I'd not be able to work that day due to illness. It was Thursday when this happened. Later that day, I received a text from him saying that I didn't need to come in on Saturday either. *What?* I called Larry in a complete panic and asked to see him ASAP. He graciously made time for me to come in the next morning. When I showed up, I was visibly hung-over and shaking from raw nerves. I'm sure he saw what a wreck I was, but he didn't say anything about my physical appearance. We talked for over an hour, but I didn't leave with much assurance about the situation. I knew something bad was going to happen — and it did.

I got fired because of my relationship with a fellow employee. It sucked; it truly devastated me. What made things worse was that our relationship ended shortly after my job did. The two seemingly positive things in my life were taken away within a matter of days, leaving me hurt and isolated.

I decided that getting out of Greenville was my best option. My best friend since elementary school, Dan, just so happened to have an empty room available in his apartment in Spartanburg. It was about thirty minutes away from my stomping grounds in Greenville. I had no job and hardly any money saved up, but I knew that I could try to get another job in Spartanburg. As soon as I got the go-ahead from Dan, I packed my things and left.

The freedom and lack of accountability was exciting. It had been quite some time since I'd been in that position — to be able to do whatever my heart desired. Dan said he would charge me a whopping fifty dollars a week to stay in the spare room.

"That's all!?" was my response.

"Yeah, I know you don't have a job right now," he said. "We can figure out the details once you get back on your feet."

"That's great, thanks so much. I'm going to get a job in the next two weeks for sure."

"I know," he said. "Take your time and find something that suits you."

We finished our conversation and went out to celebrate over some margaritas. I was really happy to be moving in with my best friend, and I could tell that he was excited too. When we got back to the apartment, I unloaded my car and brought my stuff inside. The only physical items that came with me were clothes and a computer. Bringing a bed would be too stressful, and there was not one single piece of furniture that was mine. Something about having only a few material possessions was appealing to me. I liked going rogue. I had no attachments and no responsibility — only the essentials.

When I moved in, Dan had a good job and was working like a man should. He was gone between seven a.m. and six p.m, and I was always alone during the day. There was hardly any noises or phone calls. There was no schedule and nowhere to go, only time ticking by and the heat from the summer sun that bounced off the cement. The apartment was on the third floor and the balcony that overlooked a distant highway strip quickly became my favorite spot. Cigarette after cigarette, I'd watch the cars zip by and plan my next move. I'd dream about doing something awesome, like making a good living, or possibly moving to a different country.

But, more than the desire for success was my desire to get high and take away my misery. It had been quite some time that I'd been off the Klonopin, but life wasn't much easier than when Dr. Tee first cut me off in rehab. I hated how my strong personality morphed into a passively insecure, angry one since coming off the benzos. I had no love for myself, only guilt and regret, hate and sadness. And, since I was alone for most of the day, all the garbage that ran through my head turned itself into reality. My coping mechanisms reverted back to what I use to do in those situations.

The longer I went without a job, the more weed I began to smoke. The drive to visit my dealer in Greenville was a long one, but weed and booze and whatever pills I could get my hands on topped my priority list. The liquor store also became a place that I loved going to. Usually when I drank it was beer, but the raw taste of whiskey changed my perspective when I moved to Spartanburg.

Dan asked me one day how my job search was coming. "Where have you applied at? Any leads?" His inquiry startled me. I knew that I needed a job, but it was weird for my best friend to ask me about it.

"Well, it's going. I hit up a few places here in Spartanburg, but I'm going to look in Greenville as well. There's more restaurants there."

"Cool," he said, cracking open a deserved beer and sitting down to relax. He had just gotten home from work. "Yeah, there's a lot more options in Greenville. Let me know how that goes."

"Will do," I said, trying to not sound annoyed with his prying. Dan had no idea, but my money was already at an all time low. I desperately needed a job, and fast.

The next day I drove to Greenville and applied for a few restaurant positions, but only after drinking some liquor on the way to calm my nerves. I walked into one restaurant and got hired on the spot. The restaurant was doing a massive hiring that day and my plan was to apply as a dishwasher. But, as soon as the hiring manager met with me, she said that I was overqualified and would be a server.

It was great being hired on my first day of job hunting. Suddenly things didn't seem like they would be so bad anymore. I could make a ton of money and continue to support my habits. I trained with many different servers for a whole week. My studying even continued at the apartment, but it was nearly impossible for me to retain any information. I couldn't sit still most of the time and had to smoke a couple of bowls before even attempting to learn the simplistic menu. But, once I smoked, I couldn't remember things anyway, so it was a lose-lose situation.

At the end of the week I took a written exam, but my lack of brainpower proved to be too strong. The manager had me sit at an empty bar to take the test. To my dismay, I was only able to answer a handful of questions. It was so embarrassing that I decided to sneak out of the restaurant before they noticed me leaving. The blank test came with me. Needless to say, that job ended before it even began. How embarrassing it was telling Dan that I couldn't even pass a waiter's test.

June had only just begun, and I was already flat broke. Not only was I broke, but extremely jobless and too scared to attempt finding another job. I did fill out a couple more applications, but the thought of having to deal with social anxiety again kept me from really pursing work. At the time, being broke with no stress sounded much better than having money, since money meant having to be out in public and deal with people, specifically customers.

Now, while my anxiety was a major cause of staying jobless, I mostly wanted to just get high and forget about the person I was becoming. There was one place in particular that we would always go drink at and get crazy. We being myself, the friend I was living with, and a couple of mutual friends that were raging alcoholics. Even before going to the bar, I needed to have several drinks in order to calm my nerves. I've mentioned several times in previous sections that alcohol was never my drug of choice. It really wasn't, but during the summer of 2012, it became one.

Everything I did that summer revolved around alcohol in one way or another. *Everything*. If there was ever a time in my life where I didn't care about anyone or anything, it was then. Nothing mattered to me — not people, not drugs or alcohol, not money, not faith, nothing. Emotion became just a word, but the word to describe me was numb. Numb became my life. It became the only thing worth living for. What morals I did have left flew out the window.

My issues were definitely not helping Dan. He was also going through a bit of his own emotional struggles, the root being certain family circumstances. He decided to see a psychiatrist, who prescribed him a low dose of Ativan and an SSRI anti-depressant. He didn't really like taking the Ativan, so I asked him one day for the rest of his bottle. He gave it to me, but to my disappointment there were only a couple left, which I immediately crushed and snorted. This was the third or fourth time that I had used benzos since rehab, and while the feeling was nice, it only fueled my craving for more.

"Are you going to refill the Ativan?" I asked him. On the bottle it said that there was one refill left.

"No, I don't like the way they make me feel," he said. "Plus, I'm stopping the other medicine too."

I schemed for a moment on how to phrase my next question. If I could get him to refill the bottle, there would be 90 pills for me. "I gotcha. Is there any chance you could fill it for me? I use to take Ativan for my anxiety."

Dan lit up a cigarette. I could tell he wasn't fond of the idea, so I elaborated on why he should fill it for me. "It's going to help with my anxiety for when I search for jobs and stuff. Come on man, just do me this favor."

"I really don't feel comfortable with that," he said. "That doesn't sound like a good idea."

"Oh come on, man. It's not that big of a deal," I said, verbally poking at him. He kept shaking his head, before letting out a sigh.

"Nope, can't do it," he said. "Sorry bubba."

I was furious but played it off cool. "Na, you're good bro. It's all good." I left Dan on the porch and went back inside.

That's what the rest of June looked like for me — a constant struggle to get money and find drugs. No amount of substance was able to satisfy me. The manipulation and disgusting immorality brought me to a new depth of hopelessness. All I could think about was the stupid things that I did or didn't do, the places that I went and shouldn't have gone, and the people that I tried really hard to forget about.

Ten

It was clear.

At the rate I was going, I would either be dead or in jail by the end of the summer. I decided to call Tori from treatment during the first week of July. Part of me just wanted to vent, but the other part wanted to confess that I was completely out of control and needed help. When she didn't pick up, I left her a voicemail. A few days passed before I heard from her.

Dan, myself, and couple other guys were hanging out by the pool and drinking beer on an average summer day. My phone started ringing with an unfamiliar number. Thinking it was a telemarketing call, I picked up and said "hello" and "how are you?" in Spanish.

"Is this Zach?" the lady asked. My heart jumped out of my chest. *It was Tori.* I had totally forgotten about calling her.

"Hello?" she said. I quickly hung up the phone. *You've got to be kidding me. Did I really just do that?*

I sobered up almost instantaneously and cringed while waiting for the phone to start ringing again, because I knew it would.

One minute later, still no call. Two minutes later, nothing. I walked outside the pool area and lit up a smoke — then came the ring.

"Hello?" I said in a cautious manner.

"Zach?" she said, "Is this Zach?"

"Yes, this is Zach," I replied, swallowing the lump in my throat. *Oh God, I hope she doesn't ask about the Spanish.*

"Well hey, Zach! This is Tori from Atlanta. I just got your voicemail. How are you?"

Judging from her tone, it sounded like she was actually excited to to be talking to me. I became a bit more relaxed.

"Hey, Tori. I'm doing pretty well, I suppose. I just wanted to call and say hello. It's been a while." *That was an understatement, but what else was I to say?*

"Yes, it has been a while," she replied. "I heard from Stacy just a few days after you left Charlotte. I'm sorry to hear about what happened. Are you doing okay now?"

Oh boy, she knows everything.

"Well…" My emotional recall of the last few months must have sounded manic to her. I poured out everything that was going on, especially how sick I'd been since coming off of the Klonopin. She listened patiently and, to my surprise, didn't interrupt until I was done. "…Tori, I was just too sick to learn anything at rehab. I know now that I need help, and I'm asking you if it would be possible for me to come back to treatment."

"Yeah, you were really sick," she said. "Here's what I'm going to do. I'll talk to the staff and give you a call back in a few days. If you are still serious about it, I'll try to save a bed for you."

"I am serious, Tori," I said. "Thank you very much! I'll be waiting to hear from you."

"Alright, Zach. I'll talk to you soon, bye-bye."

I hung up the phone.

Wade was right. I was sick and tired of being sick and tired. Truly, I was drained and ready for things to get better. I was ready to not have these cravings consuming my every thought and driving me to do things that I didn't want to do.

Over the next few days I willed myself to stop smoking weed. The first night I was so irritated and angry that rest avoided me completely. By the third day, I was feeling a bit better, but red wine deserved most of the credit for that. Tori kept her promise and called me four days later on Friday, July 6th.

"Hey, Zach!" Tori sounded even more excited than our first conversation. "Listen, I spoke with the staff and we are able to save you a bed if you come before Friday of next week"

"Really?" I said.

"Yes," she replied. "What do your parents think about you coming back to treatment? Have you discussed it with them?"

"Well, they want to make sure I'm serious, and I am. My dad has been finding out all the insurance information to see how many days of inpatient they will cover. Besides all that, they are in favor of it.

"Okay," Tori replied, "But, if you use between now and then we are going to have to start you in the detox unit."

"I won't," I said, knowing there was no way in hell that I'd go back down to that unit.

"Good," she said. "We will see you next Thursday. I'm really proud of you, Zach. Don't use anything for the next couple of days. Come down clean."

"I will," I said. "See you soon."

Back in Spartanburg, I told Dan about everything that had

transpired with Tori and rehab in the last few days. He was very supportive about my decision to go back to treatment, but mostly because he just wanted me to move out of his apartment, and I can't blame him for one bit. I had literally not done anything productive since moving in with him — just debauchery, drugs, and alcohol. At my lowest point, I put a knife up to my neck in front of him and said I didn't want to live anymore.

"So, you're leaving for treatment in two days?" Dan asked, carrying my computer down the stairs and to my car.

"Yep. Two days," I mumbled.

"That's good man. You gotta do what you gotta do."

"I know...I know I need help now. Take care of yourself man. I'm not sure when I'll be back in town, but let's stay in touch." I shut my passenger door and gave him a hug.

"I'll see you later," he said, as I started my car.

"You bet." I drove off.

The night before leaving for treatment, I drank a bottle of wine to try and calm my nerves. I felt absolutely no relief, but I hadn't a dime to my name and no way of getting more booze. I went to bed frustrated. When morning came, my dad drove me down to Atlanta. The time had come.

Being back in Atlanta felt weird and almost rushed, but it was also necessary. I knew that this time I would learn and get it right.

I had to go through orientation again, which was simply a list of questions and a breathalyzer test. The lady giving the orientation told us to wait in the lobby for a young adult staff member to pick me up. Thankfully, tensions weren't nearly as high between my dad and I as they were the first time. We actually embraced in a hug before he left.

Elizabeth, the receptionist of the young adult unit, drove a golf cart down to the lobby to pick me up. The smile on her face when she saw me was unforgettable. She ran up and gave me hug.

"Zach!" she said, beaming from ear to ear. "We're so glad you're back! Everyone is so excited to see you again!" Her enthusiastic embrace almost made me cry. I was expecting her to be disappointed in me, if not judgmental about my return.

"I'm happy to see you," I said, giving her yet another hug. "How is Garrett doing?" Her smile faded slightly.

"Garrett is actually counseling somewhere else," she replied. "But don't worry, you will see him soon. He comes nearly every Wednesday afternoon to lead a musical therapy session with the drums."

"Oh, okay," I replied, trying to mask my disappointment. "What about Lester? How is he doing?"

"Lester is great," she said. "We have been talking about you since Tori told us you'd be coming back."

"Oh wow," I laughed. "They aren't mad at me, are they?"

"No, of course not!" she yelled. "We are just so glad that you are coming back to get help."

Elizabeth drove me up to the young adult unit on her golf cart. You should have seen Lester's face when I walked through the doors. His infectious smile was even more welcoming than Elizabeth's. "Zach!" he yelled. "It's good to see you, baby!" He held out his massive hand and pulled me toward him for a life-crushing hug. Miss D also walked outside of her office when she heard the commotion.

The next ten minutes were overwhelming, as the good and bad memories from my first time in treatment circulated throughout my mind, giving me the nervous shakes. I went outside on the smoking patio to calm my fried nerves. The glass windows that surrounded it allowed me to look inside and see Tori, who was sitting in her office and talking on the phone. She gave me a quick smile when she saw me and put up a finger to let me know that she'd be with me in a minute. I smoked my cigarette while constantly looking up to see if she was ready to give me some attention. When her phone call was over, she came on the patio to have a chat with me.

"Well, you did it," she said. "You're here. How are you feeling?"

"I'm a little nervous, but I'm glad to be back. Thank you for giving me another chance."

Tori gave me that authoritative smile — the type that lets a person know who is really in charge. "You're going to meet with Dr. Tee this afternoon," she said. "He's excited to see you too."

I laughed. Good ol' Dr. Tee. I was ready to see him, even though he cut me off the Klonopin last time, which put me in a hellhole.

"Now Zach," Tori said softly, "We really need you to focus on both aspects during treatment. Of course, your addiction, but also whatever this mood disorder is that you have." Her bold statement took me back a second. *She's still pushing that mood disorder thing.* I had forgotten that they thought I had a mood disorder. Dr. Lord (who I saw in Charlotte) and my other doctor in Greenville didn't think so, which is why I didn't know what to believe anymore. They all had a different opinion when it came to my anxiety, but the one thing that all these doctors and counselors could agree upon was that I was an addict.

"Yeah, sure thing Tori," I said, trying to push her statement aside.

"Alright, go ahead and get settled in. I'll see you soon."

She walked back inside, leaving me alone on the patio. I tried to put her statement out of my mind, but was unsuccessful. *Do they see something that I don't? What mood disorder? Why can't I just be unique or different, or artsy for that matter.* I heard the patio door open and looked to see who it was. It was Dr. Tee.

I couldn't help but smile. "Hey Dr. Tee. Long time no see, huh?"

He chuckled, "Hey Zach, come on back and talk with me."

Dr. Tee looked the same, maybe a little wiser; he seemed to age with an intellectual look. He listened intently while I explained to him everything that had happened since leaving treatment back in December. I told him that I'd been benzo-free with the exception of a couple slip-ups.

"I'll tell you," I said, "It was hell, literally the worst thing I've ever gone through when you took me off of Klonopin. I was so, so sick, definitely unable to focus or learn anything."

He almost laughed, not because it was funny, but because everything I'd just said he already knew. He knew how dope sick I was last December. "Tell me what medications you're taking," he asked, changing the subject slightly.

"I'm still taking the Lexapro in the morning and Depakote

twice a day, but that's about it. The Hydroxyzine for anxiety was not really working." I waited to see what he would say, if he wanted to change or tweak any of the medicine.

"Well, have you ever been on Buspar?" he asked. "It has a similar GABA effect like benzos do, but its non-habit forming and very safe. I think if we start that twice a day it will really help reduce your anxiety." He stopped taking notes and looked up at me to study my reaction.

"Yeah, I'm not opposed to that," I replied. "What about Inderal? Would it be possible to take that as well? I remember how it helped me function better in social situations."

"Do you know why that is?" he asked rhetorically. "It keeps your heart rate down which prevents panic attacks and some of the physical symptoms of anxiety, like sweating or redness. But yes, I can also give you a low dose of Inderal in the mornings and afternoons. We'll evaluate in a few days."

"Okay, that works for me."

He folded his notepad, which meant our meeting was coming to a close. I could tell that he wasn't nearly as concerned with me as the last time, which in itself was a confidence booster. It made me feel like I'd made at least *some* kind of progress handling my anxiety.

The next morning I started group therapy again. My new counselor's name was Shelly. She was feisty, in her early forties, and very experienced with addiction as she herself was an alcoholic — a sober alcoholic. Shelly put a big emphasis on having a higher power of your choosing. This higher power could really be *anything*, or at least that's what I gathered. This one guy named Ham had a door knob as his higher power, which seemed humorous, but understandable since he was an atheist.

Shelly was also a big fan of the twelve step program in A.A., and she encouraged all of us to get a temporary sponsor while in treatment. The A.A. and N.A. meetings we went to at night were open to the public, and a lot of the alumni would come and offer to sponsor the addicts currently in treatment. At this stage in my life, I wanted to try new things. I wanted to explore this A.A. stuff and learn all I could about it. While I didn't like the meetings in Charlotte, the meetings on campus here in Atlanta were fascinating and full of young adults and teens.

The clearest memories from my second stay in treatment were absolutely these A.A. meetings. They were held at night in a big building near the entrance of the treatment facility. It was fun to see all the units (young adult, adult, adolescent) come together at the end of the day and support one another. There were even alumni from my first time in treatment still coming back to these meetings on campus. One guy in particular stood out to me. He was a wreck when we went through treatment together. His OCD and guilt from the things he had done were eating him alive. Now, he was a new man and I hardly recognized him. He looked about the same physically, but emotionally he was completely stable. His confidence and inner-peace radiated off of him like I could not believe. I wanted that confidence, that charisma which was so inviting.

I too was in a much better place emotionally this second time in treatment. It was not nearly as difficult to listen to Shelly's therapy sessions, or make it through a typical day for that matter. Conversations came to me easier, anger fled more quickly, and hope seemed closer. For the first time in a very *long* time, I was motivated. I was driven to succeed and make something of myself.

- After Three Weeks of Treatment -

It might have been my imagination, but I could feel the staff slowly wean me off of them. I was no longer their biggest concern. Narcissistic? Perhaps, but this was territory I'd not seen in quite some time. I knew what I had to do — it was time to move on. It was time for that next step: Progress. That scared the hell into me. Staying in the depths had become comfortable. If it was time for that next step and I *had* to progress, there would be a possibility that I would fail. This was when my anxiety would show itself. *What if I was not able to get a job? What if my anxiety prevents me from functioning? What if I never get off of these medicines? What am I supposed to do in Atlanta?* What ifs.

My parents agreed that a sober living house *in* Atlanta would be beneficial after completing the program. We both knew I needed to be close to the treatment facility, the staff, and the friends here in treatment. Tori took me aside one morning and informed me that I should set up an interview with the sober living house.

"You won't be here too much longer," she said, "maybe a couple more weeks."

Eleven

Once again, my interview with the leaders of the sober living program didn't take place until my last week of treatment. Since leaving the campus wasn't an option, they came to me for our interview. I was nervous, but it was a good meeting and I liked them from the start. They were curious to hear some of my story and all the progress I'd made in the last five weeks. We must have talked for at least an hour. When our meeting came to a close, they invited me to enter their program. They said I would be living in one of their houses in Dunwoody, twenty minutes away from the treatment campus. I was glad to hear that it wasn't too far away. Tori, Shelly, Dr. Tee, and the staff would be close by if anything were to go terribly wrong. Not that I was planning on it, but the safety net was a relief.

My mind seemed to skip to the future as if the present was already past. The last few days went by with a quickness; the graduation ceremony is the last clear memory I have. Lester gave a long motivational speech like he did for all of the addicts when they graduate. He talked about persevering through the hard times and ended the ceremony by saying, "Zach, we need people like you." I don't know exactly what he meant, but it had a positive impact on me. I can still picture him saying it — facial expressions and all.

I said my goodbyes to the staff as casually as possible. I tried to not make a big deal about it because I knew that I would be coming back to visit with them. Dr. Tee wrote several extra prescriptions and said I could fill them at the campus pharmacy for the first couple of months, or until I found another doctor in Atlanta.

My parents drove me to my new residence in Dunwoody. It was quite an experience driving through the highway traffic on interstate 285. Things were moving fast, much faster than the daily pace I was use to in rehab. The amount of traffic was ridiculous, but it wasn't just the cars or the hustle and bustle — it was the real world that caught me off-guard. A wave of anxiety came over me, making me feel slightly nauseated. The realization that I was actually taking that next step set in quickly on the drive.

When we pulled into the driveway and I went inside, it was clear that my experience here would *not* be the same as it was in Charlotte. Everything about the house and program was older and rougher, completely opposite from the apartments in Drew's program. Upon first glance, most of the men were in their twenties. Of course, there was the usual exception of a couple older men. Unlike the program in Charlotte, completing treatment was not a necessity to live here. Some of the addicts came from jail, some from their daily lives, and others, like myself, came straight from treatment.

My parents said goodbye and I was left to begin my new life.

I sat down with Jake, a leader of the house, and we went over the house rules. He made me feel welcome and I liked his spastic energy. My first impression of him was similar to Drew.

"Tell me about yourself, Zach." he said, twirling a pen around in his hand.

"I'm nervous," I said. "Everything's a bit overwhelming. I just left treatment today."

"Yeah, that's what they told me," he said. "There's some good guys in here, and we all stick together. Here's my number. Give me a call if you need anything."

"Thanks, I appreciate that." I replied, typing his number into my phone.

"Alright, now for the boring stuff," Jake laughed, sliding some papers under my nose. He went on to tell me more about the daily life in the house and what my focus should be while I was in the program. All of their recovery protocol was based on A.A. literature and the twelve steps. Jake said that we were required to go to at least six meetings a week, meet with our sponsors, and work the twelve steps consistently. Sobriety was absolutely priority number one. Priority number two was getting and keeping a job. It didn't have to be a full-time career, just something that would keep us busy and help us learn responsibility again. Idle hands were the last thing that they wanted us to have.

Since I was still certified as a personal trainer, my job search consisted of locating all the gyms in Dunwoody. There were a few that caught my eye. I was then faced with the inevitable challenge of introducing myself and dropping off resumes.

Something about living in an area where I had a fresh slate allowed me to focus more on the present and not worry as much about my shady track record in the fitness industry. I called all the gyms once a week to make sure they had not forgotten about me. My persistence paid off, and within a few weeks a gym hired me on as a trainer.

Again, life was in a progressive phase for me. I worked at the gym, went to my meetings with friends in the program, and enjoyed seeing more of the city life in Atlanta. The longer I stayed out in public, the easier it was to handle worry and social anxieties. No, it wasn't always easy living in a house with five other guys. We were all addicts trying to stay sober amidst each other's varying work schedules and personal obstacles. The tension was palpable at times.

A handful of guys relapsed within my first two months in the program. Unlike at treatment, it seemed a lot more "normal" when somebody would go out and use. My friends who had been living there the longest were very accustomed to it. Literally, within an hour the addict that had relapsed was no longer the topic of discussion. It was as if our attitude was, "better you than me." It's not that we didn't care, but if you are constantly worrying about your own sobriety, how can you worry about others too? Since our lives were still unmanageable, it was impossible to dwell on that relational dynamic. The only addicts that did seem to be concerned were the leaders of the program and our personal A.A. sponsors.

I had started working the steps with my sponsor shortly after moving into the house. His name was Caleb; he was an alumnus from rehab. He was a year older than me and also worked as a personal trainer. Caleb was extremely blunt and took the A.A. program *very* seriously, but that's why I asked him to be my sponsor in the first place. I remember approaching him at a meeting in treatment and saying, "Hey, I'm wondering if you would like to be my sponsor. You don't seem like the kind of guy who puts up with nonsense." He responded with an entertained laugh. Then he said, "Yeah, actually you are right, and I will be your sponsor."

When I left treatment shortly thereafter, I called Caleb and told him I was ready to start working the steps.

"Great," he said. "Let's do this."

We started meeting once a week to read the big book and discuss the program. We would meet at a coffee shop and sit outside smoking cigarettes and drinking espresso. Working the A.A. steps goes in order with the book, so we started from the beginning and worked our way *slowly,* taking time to hit the symbolism and highlights of each chapter. I enjoyed reading through the big book with him while sharing my personal insecurities with recovery. The revitalization that I felt after our meetings was satisfying, even if only for a few hours. The feeling was the same after A.A. meetings. I went, sat down, listened, spoke, and left. If I started the meeting with any sort of craving, it was truly gone afterwards.

It seems that life always has a way of distracting you from what's worth pursuing. In my case, it was work and a girl. The more time I spent working and hanging out with her, the less I desired to meet with Caleb. My excuse to him was always work related. Relationships for newly sober addicts are a touchy subject and I didn't want to mention this girl to him just yet. My procrastination to meet with him continued until, eventually, all contact had ceased. Caleb never called to check in or see how I was doing, but I expected that. In the A.A. program, it's the sponsee's duty to call his or her sponsor.

It still made me feel worthless when he wouldn't call or shoot me a text to see if I was still alive. The last time we spoke, I expressed my desire to look for another sponsor. Clearly unaware of my true reasons, he told me that he understood and said to call him sometime, but I never did.

Instead of looking for a new sponsor, I tried to pursue a relationship with my co-worker. She was a lot of fun to be with and much more appealing than reading the big book. Soon enough, my number one priority had fallen down my short list of responsibilities. I still went to my A.A. meetings because they were a requirement, but after another month they started to feel like a chore.

After ten weeks of living in Dunwoody, the leaders moved me to their other house in Doraville — about five miles away. Jake was the one who informed me of the change. I knew the guys that lived there because we were all in the same program. Even so, I wasn't thrilled about leaving my friends in the first house. They had become like family to me. In this new house were three guys that had been roommates together for quite some time. Since I was the odd man out, it took a while to get settled in and feel "at home" so to speak. Truthfully, I never did completely feel at home. I missed my friends at the other house. I missed the location, and I missed feeling like I belonged. In retrospect, a lot more could have been done on my part to get involved with these guys, but the complacency in my sobriety had a lot to do with it.

Continuously dwelling on my miserable surroundings led *me* to feeling miserable, which led to my old patterns of anger and bitterness. There were many times when I'd go to the liquor store and buy airplane bottles of whiskey, then sit in my car and debate for half an hour on whether or not I would drink them. It would have been easy to get away with, but the thought of having to be dishonest again was even more unappealing than having to deal with my miserable circumstances. I stayed clean for nearly two months before relapsing in Charlotte. I was well past that mark now and did *not* want to forfeit the accomplishment.

This inner debate of mine would always end with the bottles being tossed out of the window. Instead of drinking, I bought a portable cd player and began listening to motivational speakers talk about how to change your attitude and rise out of the dumps. Over and over and over I listened to these four messages. Every single night and occasionally in the afternoon I would put on my headphones and get lost in this dream of hope. The ritual kept me distracted from how desperate I was to get out of my current situation. What I failed to accept was that my present circumstances were only temporary. *Would I really be in a halfway house forever? Working a dead end job forever? Living with cravings forever?* No, I wouldn't, but all good things take time; instant gratification was still what I wanted most.

One weekend in late November, I decided to take a trip back to Greenville and visit my family. Before we could leave the house overnight, we had to put in a request form and meet with a leader to discuss our plans and how to handle temptations or cravings if they were to occur. It wasn't the first leave I had taken since moving into the halfway house, so I didn't worry too much about craving or relapsing. I should have.

It was a Friday evening when I went back to Greenville. Nighttime had fallen, but the liquor store by my parents house was still open. The thought of going inside and looking around at the alcohol was too exciting to pass up. I wasn't going to *buy* anything; I just wanted to feel normal again, free again, not restricted from doing as my heart pleased. The clerk, Robert, hadn't seen me in quite sometime, but immediately he recognized my face and was very eager to ask where I'd been and what I'd been doing with my life. My answer was, "I've been living in Atlanta and working down there."

Talking with Robert brought back memories of when I would visit him and buy my whiskey. He was such a kind person and always greeted me with a smile. More importantly, he always remembered our previous conversations and would pick right back up from where we left off. I wondered why he was even working in a place like this. Robert was the man — a liquor store did not suit his personality.

Suddenly it felt weird that I should be in there talking with him, but then leave without buying anything. *Who does that?*

I ended up leaving with several small bottles of whiskey. It felt very human to walk out with that brown paper bag. I enjoyed listening to the crinkling noise the bag made as I caressed the curves of the bottles inside. *No, I won't drink them*, I told myself. *It's just for fun and comfort.*

The next few hours went by slowly, during which I mostly held the bottles and stared at their golden hues. *What if I just smell it? I won't drink it, I just want to smell it.* I went upstairs and got a small glass, filled it with the airplane bottle of whiskey, smelled it, then set it down on my desk. Thirty minutes went by with the golden glass looking back at me. I smelled it a few more times — each time my nose came closer to the rim of the glass. *They will never know, just have a sip.* Quickly, before my mind could respond again, I picked up the glass and poured it into my mouth. *Should I swallow it? Technically I haven't relapsed yet.* My throat was fighting the urge to swallow the whiskey, but it was a little too late.

Twelve

The liquor store was already closed by the time the small bottles of whiskey were gone; cheap beer from a gas station was all that was available. I felt ashamed about drinking at my parents house of all places, but equally satisfied to be chasing this pleasure secretly with such drive and focus. I knew that my manipulative switch had been turned on. It was the other side of me — the side that would tear me apart piece by piece.

My trip was cut short because I couldn't even look my parents in the eye, much less have a meaningful conversation with them. There was just too much anxiety to pretend like nothing had happened. All of it had been brought on by my own choices; I was well aware of that.

On the way back to Atlanta, I debated on whether or not it would be a good idea to tell the leaders of the program about my relapse. On one hand, they would never find out if I chose not to say anything. On the other hand, *could I really keep this a secret?* Was I still sick enough that I'd be able to repress it, hide it, bury it deep down and forget it ever happened? This back and forth in my head consumed the three-hour drive. My final decision was made at the very last second when I pulled into the driveway in Doraville. Since getting kicked out of the house was *not* an option, my relapse would have to remain a secret. No one could know but me.

That was much easier said than done. The weight of that secret ate at me continuously for a solid week. I wanted to tell someone, but I knew that confessing my relapse to the leaders meant leaving the house for at least a month. It was my own damn fault, so I couldn't be mad at anyone but me.

I tried to be excited — excited that I could start drinking again guilt-free if they kicked me out. My twisted logic allowed me to feel better about myself by putting the blame on them instead of something that I'd done. It became a sudden revelation. Confessing *was* the answer!

I called Jake and said, "We need to talk about something." He already knew, and I knew that he did. It was absolutely no surprise to him when I mentioned the relapse that happened during my trip to Greenville. You should have seen Jake's face. He wasn't disappointed, angry, upset, happy, worried, or anything. His reaction was no different than if I had told him the current temperature outside.

"Well, you know we have to ask you to leave for thirty days," he said.

"Yeah, I know," I muttered.

"You can stay the night if you need to, but tomorrow morning you gotta go."

"That's okay," I replied, "I'm leaving for Greenville tonight." It was already almost midnight, but that didn't matter. The bar would still be open when I got back.

"Alright. Well call me soon, okay? You have my number."

"Yeah, I do," I replied. "I'm going back to the house to pack my things and say goodbye to the guys."

We embraced in a quick hug, and then I went back to the house and said my goodbyes. I also drove back to the house in Dunwoody to tell my *closest* friends the news. They were sad to see my go and vice versa, but it wasn't too difficult to say goodbye; I had been away from them for a while. Had I still been living in the same house with them, it probably would have been *very* difficult. Inevitably, it turned out to be a blessing.

With my goodbyes out of the way, I had nothing more to do but drive back to Greenville. To my delight, the bars were still open when I got back. It felt good to be able to drink publicly without worrying about getting caught, but the drinks didn't satisfy me as planned. It was fun for one whole hour, but it just wasn't enough — not even close to being enough.

By the next day my parents had learned from the leaders of the program that I'd relapsed and was asked to leave the house. They were furious. In fact, they told me not to even *think* about trying to come back home. *Good*, I thought. *They will just keep guilt tripping me and make me feel horrible about myself, which I don't need right now.*

Since my options were limited, I decided to go to the library and look for jobs online, which turned out to be completely pointless. I had no resume, no patience to make one, no place to stay, hardly any money, and nowhere to go. Honest to God I've never felt more childish in my entire life. I felt like a twenty-two year old kid. It never occurred to me how dependent I was on my parents to bail me out of my self-destructive situations. I was humiliated but too proud in the moment to admit my mistakes, especially to my family. I left the library in disgust.

I had three hundred dollars to my name, which I felt could be best used towards beer and hotels. This would buy me some more time to figure out a plan. I went to my favorite place to drink, which was actually a restaurant. I sat at the bar because you could smoke there. I drank for a solid hour, then went to the bathroom and vomited so my binging could continue. This drink-vomit-drink cycle had always been an issue for me, but it got worse as my drinking progressed. The worst part of it was having to wait in the bathroom for my blood-shot eyes to turn white again. Otherwise the bartender wouldn't serve me any more drinks.

When my tab reached a certain number, I called it quits and left. The next twenty-four hours, as you could probably guess, were somewhat questionable. An old friend of mine was still living in Greenville, so we linked up and got a hotel for the night. We drank and drank, snorted Klonopin, and drank some more. The resulting blackout scared me. We awoke to the sound of the hotel owner banging on our door and yelling for us to get out. It was close to noon and we didn't even know what day it was, or really what was going on at all. Still half drunk and high, we stumbled out of the hotel and drove away.

I eventually dropped him off somewhere and began driving to my next unknown destination. My phone buzzed from a text as I was driving around aimlessly — it was my mother. She said that she spoke with the leader in Dunwoody and he had recommended another halfway house in Sandy Springs, just down the road from them. I read the text slowly, absorbing every word and letting the letters sink into my brain. Before I had time to respond to her, my phone buzzed again. It was my dad this time. "Come to the house and let's talk about it," he said in the text. I decided to hear them out and hopefully, if anything, get some rest.

That was actually the first thing I did — sleep. When I woke up several hours later, the Klonopin had worn off and the rebound anxiety was in full swing. My hands were shaking and my brain was racing. I felt like complete shit, but fortunately there were a few more pills in my jacket pocket left over from the previous night. I quickly crushed one and snorted it as fast as possible.

Complete silence.

The longer I sat there in silence, the stronger the relief was and the quicker my brain leveled out. I wanted this feeling to last forever, but eventually I had to go upstairs and talk with my parents about the other halfway house in Atlanta. I remember exactly where they were sitting and what time of day it was, but not a lot of what was said during our discussion. I'll blame this on the Klonopin.

Basically, they asked me to think it over and let them know in a few hours if I was willing to check into another sober living program. If my decision *were* to go, the lady in charge would need to know that night, and the next morning I would have to go back to Atlanta. Time was of the essence. I went downstairs to think for a few hours, which honestly wasn't necessary. My decision was absolutely to go to this new halfway house and force myself back into sobriety. I wanted to forget about my humiliating conquests since returning to Greenville. My slow and steady growth over the past four months had been unnoticeable to me at the time, but now that I was back in the depths again, it was clear. I didn't realize that living sober and honest had provided such a blanket of security. I wanted that feeling back, and I wanted my anxiety gone.

The next morning I quickly said goodbye to whatever family

was at the house, then drove with a purpose to get out of Greenville and back to safety. One of the two leaders of the new halfway house met me outside of the apartment. I saw a lady out on the sidewalk and hoped to God it wasn't the leader I was meeting.

Thirteen

Her name was Debra. She was a petite lady, but her piercing dark eyes and spiky jet-black hair made up for her lack of stature. Her leathery tan skin and raspy voice furthered the intimidation factor. She didn't look like she would be a pushover, but she did look like an alcoholic. The years and years of drinking were not merciful to Debra, that much was clear.

"Are you Zach?" she asked harshly.

I stepped out of the car. "Hi, yes I am," I replied.

Debra stayed put as she smothered a cigarette between her fingers and the wet steps. She waited for *me* to take that long walk to her and introduce myself. As I approached her, I held out my hand in peace.

"I'm Debra, nice to meet you," she said. "Come inside and let's have a little chat."

I followed Debra up the wooden stairs to the apartment door. She took out a key ring that must have had thirty to fifty color coded keys on it. It was obvious that she was a seasoned veteran, and it took her less than five seconds to identify the right key and fling the door open like she owned the place.

"Have a seat," she said. "We have to go over some paperwork, but first you're going to tell me why you are here and what happened recently at the other place." Her bold question startled me. I was left to answer her vulnerable and uncalculated.

"Well, uh…I was doing really well at the other halfway house, but I slipped up in Greenville with some Klonopin and booze." I applauded myself for answering Debra so simply. It was the cold hard truth.

"Well, were you working the twelve steps with a sponsor?" she asked. Her question was undoubtedly rhetorical.

"No, I wasn't," I replied. "I did have a sponsor at one point, but we never got past the first couple of steps."

"Well, that's going to have to change," Debra huffed. "To stay sober, you have to go to meetings, meet with your sponsor, AND work through the twelve steps. If you're going to be in our program, you should know that we require the guys and girls to go to six meetings a week. Three of those meetings have to be at the clubhouse right down the road. We have sheets that you must get signed after every meeting by an A.A. member."

I nodded as she continued with the rules. "Every Monday and Thursday night you are required to go to a check-up meeting with all the men in the program. Rod is the men's leader here and he runs those meetings; you'll meet him soon enough. We also drug test twice a week. When we're done talking I'll give you the first one. If you test positive for benzos or whatever else, you have one week before we will test you again. And it had better be clean, or your ass is out of here." A smirk came across my face; her transparency was refreshing.

"What are the rules about getting a job?" I asked. "How much time do I have to find one?"

"It's supposed to be within two weeks, but if we see you are doing well and making a solid effort, we will extend that by a week or two."

I let out an anxious sigh, but I couldn't let Debra see my fear. I had a feeling she would eat me alive if she did.

"Now, I've gone over most of the rules, and the others you will learn as you go. If you agree to all this, we can finish the paperwork."

"Yes, of course," I replied.

"Good," she said, sliding the papers across the table.

I finished signing all the necessary documents and then took the initial drug test. A few minutes later she came back and said, "Yep, you tested positive for benzos. You've got one week, buddy."

"I know," I said. "I don't want to get back on those things anyway."

She didn't say anything; actions always speak louder than words. As far as she knew, I was a still a liar, thief, and a cheat. I couldn't blame her one bit.

"Go ahead and get settled in," she said. "I'll be back in a couple of hours to give you a meeting sheet and your key."

"Alright, thanks Debra."

As soon as she left, I went to my room and pulled out some clean clothes. I looked like hell and needed to shower and shave, badly. That was hands-down the best shower I have ever taken in my life. All of the physical gunk washed off, but so did the shame and guilt that had built up over my hellacious weekend. I hopped out feeling like a new man. Even Debra noticed, when she came back an hour later.

"Wow, you look totally different! Much better." It was the first time I'd seen her smile.

"Thank you," I laughed. "I feel much, much better."

As quickly as her smile appeared, it vanished.

"Alright, well here's your meeting sheet and key to the apartment. You should go to a meeting at the clubhouse this afternoon. The 5:15 is a popular one for our guys; so you should probably go to that one and introduce yourself, maybe even find a sponsor. And don't forget the other men's meeting at 7:15. It's in apartment 401A."

"Will do," I replied.

"You have my number. Call me if you need anything," she said as she walked towards the door. I nodded, then she left.

For the next few hours, I unpacked my things and went grocery shopping at the Kroger down the street. After that, I took Debra's advice and went up to the clubhouse for the 5:15 meeting. I sat by myself, but there were multiple A.A. members that I recognized from other meetings scattered throughout metro Atlanta. When it was over, I went back to my apartment to get ready for the check up meeting with Rod and the other men in the program. I carefully followed the map Debra gave me to the apartment.

The meeting took place in the living room, which was about as crammed as you'd expect a two-bedroom apartment to be. Rod was there with most of the men, minus the predictable stragglers in every program. He didn't say much to me before the meeting started. It might have been because new guys were always coming into the program, or quite possibly he was just a man of few words. Either way, I believe the most he gave me was a "Hi" and a handshake.

Rod had a look about him that was very serious and re-
served; I could tell he was a deep thinker. He was soft-spoken,
but his tone was tense for being so quiet. He had mannerisms
of a person easily agitated, with the self-control to not raise
his voice. I couldn't tell at the time if he was the most stable
or unstable addict I'd ever met. Either way, he had my respect.

I wasn't nervous when the meeting began. Everything felt
routine, which is almost depressing in and of itself. However,
as the meeting progressed into issues of substance, I found
that I was completely mistaken to believe this program would
be the same as the one in Dunwoody. It was not the same;
they were all different.

The men seemed to take their sobriety extremely seriously.
They seemed driven to succeed, not only from fear of what
would happen if they relapsed, but also from their haunting
pasts. You could hear regret and remorse in the tone of their
voices; it was something that I knew all too well. Rod was
generous to the guys with his praise after they spoke, but his
bluntness was enough to make you think twice about what
was coming out of your mouth. I found myself captivated
every time he talked during the meeting. He was just that kind
of speaker.

I felt refreshed once the meeting was over. I even spent con-
siderable time talking with the addicts after the meeting, including my two roommates who had been at work earlier. It
was a good first day.

For the rest of the week I went to meetings, explored the
new area, and worked on my resume. There were several gyms
in Sandy Springs I applied at for a personal trainer position,

but each one of them required a degree in exercise science, along with a national certification. I had the certification, but definitely no degree. Since I had already burned my bridge at the gym in Dunwoody, it was time to completely change my resume and job search. My qualifications went from personal trainer to cook/server/customer service. It was quite drastic, I know, but the food industry was the only other area that I had work experience in. Even so, Debra and Rod did NOT play games, so having *any* job would be better than having no job and getting kicked out of the program.

When I wasn't on my daily job search, most of my free time was spent at the clubhouse. There was something about those meetings that I just couldn't get enough of — stress relief. This release came *after* the meeting ended, and it felt amazing to walk out with a clear and focused mind. I felt no cravings or worry about the future. After each meeting my self-confidence would soar and my social anxieties would digress ever so slightly. My circumstances were improving and I was becoming a believer in these A.A. meetings.

I even got a callback for a job interview. The timeframe was just under the two-week mark required by Debra and Rod. It was a Kroger in Marietta, about fifteen minutes away from Sandy Springs. When I went in for my job interview something amazing happened. I was calm, not shaking, not sweating, focused, and sharp as a tack. For the first time in my life, I *completely* nailed an interview. After just a few short minutes of talking, the interviewing manager said, "Okay, I'm going to drug test you now." Without breaking eye contact or even moving a muscle, I smiled and said, "Alright, that sounds great." It did sound great because I was clean, as clean as you could possibly be. The same interviewing manager called me back within the week and asked when I could start training.

"As soon as possible," I replied.

"How does Monday morning sound?" he asked.

"Perfect, I'll be there. Thanks again," I said, trying to contain my excitement. I had to tell someone immediately. Debra was nearby, so she was the first person who heard about my success. She was thrilled as well, and informed me that she too had worked for Kroger when she first got sober and was living in a halfway house.

I told the rest of the guys about my success during one of our men's meetings with Rod. I'm sure they could feel my excitement. I honestly did not care in the least what my career status was or what this job required of me. Just the fact that I would be working and receiving a paycheck each week was enough. It was a huge boost of motivation for me to keep doing the right thing.

After only one week of training, I started working four to five days a week, consistently. My schedule stayed full and almost every week was identical, both in work and recovery. I actually enjoyed the structured feeling of purpose that Debra and Rod implemented through the rules, chores, and house meetings. It was a relief to have a routine, even if it was stressful at times. In the blink of an eye, I had once again achieved sixty days of sobriety! It felt beyond satisfying to pick up that chip and see Debra sitting in the front row, just beaming from ear to ear. She was so proud of me; that's what she said afterwards.

Even though all of my hard work and persistence was paying off, I was still missing something. My outward demeanor didn't show it, but loneliness and the uncertainty of life started to consume my joy. I found it more and more challenging to live in the moment; I wanted to feel loved and comforted. I wanted to know that my life would get better one day. I wouldn't be stuck in this halfway house forever.

A simple solution that seemed to work quite well was listening to podcasts a couple of times each week. They were comforting and combatted the loneliness that I so desperately hated. Most of the time they were messages from a church back in South Carolina. There was a whole list of podcasts to choose from, but I mostly listened to the messages that had a familiar title: anxiety, being overwhelmed, depression or failure. If podcasting wasn't an option, I would just pray. *Help me God. If You are real, show me who You are and what to do.*

On one seemingly normal day, I overheard a big rumor going around that Debra — yes Debra — had relapsed. My first thought was that it couldn't be true. She was a drill sergeant and way too confident in her sobriety to have relapsed. However, when I didn't see her around the apartments or clubhouse in the following days, my mind started to think that it was true.

At the beginning of the next men's meeting, Rod opened up with, "I'm sure most of you have heard the rumor about Debra relapsing. Several days ago I visited with her and she agreed to a drug test, which came back positive." The room was dead silent. Rod continued with, "I have asked her to step down temporarily until we figure out what the best option is for you guys and our program."

Out of all people, Debra was the *last* person that we expected to relapse. She seemed so secure in her sobriety. The way in which she gave us advice and talked in a semi-demeaning way made all of us believe that she was unbreakable. At the following men's meeting, she actually came and spoke to us, but it wasn't the Debra that we knew. In walked a scared, worried, visibly tired and tormented addict.

"I took Valium," she said while crying. "I'm so, so sorry that I let you guys down." She took a second to wipe away some emotionally heavy tears. "I'm going to pick up a white chip tomorrow night at the clubhouse. It would mean a lot if you guys could come support me." All of us nodded our heads — some empathically, others because of the palpable pressure from Rod's eyes.

Debra left a few minutes later and Rod opened up the meeting for everyone to share their thoughts on the matter. Since she *was* the CFO of the program, some of the guys didn't want to give her their rent money now that she'd relapsed, which I thought was a little overboard. Several more men shared their opinion on the matter, but the long breaks of silence seemed to prevail. Rod was visibly tense. He didn't seem concerned for Debra's sake; it was more like he was mad that his program was now in jeopardy of becoming tarnished.

The following night, we all went to the clubhouse to support Debra and watch her pick up another white chip. People from all over metro Atlanta came to be a part of her new beginning, and if I recall correctly, there were more people at this specific meeting than at any other I'd been to. It was difficult to even find a seat. Debra sat with her head either in her hands or leaned up against one of her friend's shoulders. *Poor Debra*, I honestly did feel for her. She had lost ten years of sobriety. *Ten.* And now, even newly sober addicts like myself had more time than her! When someone first brought that to my attention it was hard to comprehend. I mean, yeah, technically since she just relapsed I had more time than her, *but really?* What I didn't understand was why the other addicts, including Debra, acted like that decade of sobriety was completely washed away. Was it?

It was Debra that I saw at the clubhouse more than anyone else in the following week. She must have been going to at least three meetings a day. We talked on a few occasions, but I didn't even know this person. I wanted Debra back — confident Debra, bold Debra, punch-you-in-the-face Debra, any other Debra than the shriveled up weakling she'd become. It's sad to say, but at the time I too lost respect for her.

Debra had to step down from her leadership position in the program. When she did, Rod seemed to slack off a bit from his domineering attitude. He knew that at any time one of us could bring up what had happened and he would be stuck. Hypocrisy seemed to bother Rod, and now that it could be thrown back into his face, he was a bit of a different man.

I didn't like all the drama. I hated change, and I hated that my security in the program had been shaken. I became very bitter towards both Debra *and* Rod, and I started to pursue work instead of my sobriety. One skipped meeting turned into two, and forged signatures started to become part of my regular routine. My resentments and bitterness toward Debra started to turn on my own sobriety. I was angry that I couldn't drink alcohol. I knew without a shadow of a doubt that I was a drug addict. But no, there was no way that I would give up drinking too for the rest of my life. It's too much. Simply put,

I could not imagine going home after a hard day's work and not being able to have a beer or two. *As long as I'm working full-time and talking care of business, I can enjoy some drinks. It's time to move on.* Combine all of these three feelings and what you have is an addict who wants to get OUT of sober living and move on with life. I had just been given full-time hours and even had a place to stay if I left the program. I decided that it was time to move on.

On my very last night in the apartment, I sat down with Rod to give him the news and explain why I'd be leaving the program. He walked into my room and shut the door.

"What's up?" he asked, "What's going on?"

It took me a minute to work up the courage to voice what I was actually feeling. "Well, I'm leaving tomorrow morning," I said in my most serine tone. "Honestly Rod, I just don't think that I'm an alcoholic."

Rod put his head down for a moment, as if to search for the right words to reply with. "Do you think you're an addict?" he asked, matching my facade of serenity.

"Yes," I said, "I know for a fact that I'm an addict."

I waited for him to say, "if you're an addict, you're also an alcoholic," but he didn't. He simply nodded his head in a way that agreed, but completely disagreed. I reached over and handed him my apartment key. "Thank you for everything, Rod."

He smiled. "I enjoyed having you here, Zach," he said in an unusually disappointed tone. "Stay in touch, best of luck to you."

This caught me off guard. I expected him to be angry, but

he sounded upset and maybe even a little bit concerned. *He actually cares? No Rod, be angry like I need you to be!*

Our conversation ended shortly thereafter. We stood up, shook hands, and he even gave me a hug. Then he left, shutting the door behind him. I sat on my bed in silence, feeling proud that I spoke my mind to Rod. I also felt foolish for thinking he would react in an angry or predictable way. But, at least it was over and I was ready. Ready to leave. Ready to live. Ready to move on to a normal life.

I packed my bags in the morning and left the apartment to move in with my co-worker, Lynne. She was well aware of my reasons for wanting to leave the sober living environment before I moved in with her. I explained everything: my reservations for alcohol, the daily life of the apartments, the meetings (both A.A. and house), the leaders, and my personal goal of moving on from the restrictive lifestyle. She was a bit hesitant at first, but I assured her that I'd be safe from the slippery slope.

Let me tell you a little bit about Lynne. Having migrated down south, she was a fellow Yankee. She was full of northern swag and positive fire. To this day, I've never met anyone with such grit, such determination, such work ethic and mental toughness. She would do whatever it took to provide for herself and her family. Her house was also — conveniently — less than a mile away from the Kroger where we both worked. Lynne had two teenagers, and the two other rooms in the house were both occupied by tenets. *My* designated living area was the basement and couch. I knew it wasn't easy for her, but it was an extra four hundred dollars that she couldn't refuse, and a fresh start for myself. We both agreed to re-evaluate the situation after a month.

I quickly fell off the wagon to pursue my love of alcohol, but in the following weeks my self-control proved to be strong. It was thrilling to be able to crush a forty-hour work week, then relax at night with some drinks. I was even venturing out a little bit, enjoying some nightlife at a local bar. It was a great spot, close to my house and far enough away from Sandy Springs that I didn't worry about running into people from the program. Here's the truly great part; *nothing bad happened*. Besides getting overly drunk a few times and having to deal with a hangover, there were little, if any, consequences from my drinking. In fact, my performance at work improved and relationships with my Kroger family grew stronger. They were a ton of fun to be around — not perfect, but far more enjoyable than the egg-shell environment of sober living. Within a matter of days, I had almost completely cut off contact with my friends in recovery.

Two weeks after moving in with Lynne, I went back to the clubhouse on a whim to see if I had missed out on anything big. It was a random decision. It wasn't a planned last meeting for me, but my conversation with Debra provided me with that little extra push I wanted to completely leave those rooms.

I stepped out of my car and started walking towards the doors. Debra took a puff of her smoke and eyed me carefully when I walked up to say hello. "Hey, Debra." I said with a forced smile.

It wasn't returned. She stood there smoking for a moment before replying, "I heard from Rod that you don't think you're an alcoholic." Of course she was going to bring that up. I knew it, and I was ready.

"Yeah, I don't think I am, Debra," I replied.

"Well," she said, not looking me in the eyes, "If you're an addict, you're an alcoholic." There it was — the inevitable remark. We stood there in silence until one of us had to walk away from the awkwardness.

"Alright, Debra. It was good to see you. Take care." I went inside to the meeting. It was the last time we spoke. There was nothing more I wanted from that clubhouse, or Rod and Debra for that matter. They made me angry and bitter, a feeling that I'd always had a hard time processing. My natural instinct was to run away from confrontation, so that's what I did.

When the month at Lynne's house was up, my own evaluation determined that I had to find a place with my own room. I enjoyed living with Lynne and was so grateful that she gave me a chance. But, now it was time to move on to a better living situation.

A private room became available with yet another co-worker at Kroger. This time I had a huge queen bed, a private bathroom, and, in general, way more privacy. Rent was three hundred dollars a month, utilities included. It seemed to be an absolutely positive step in the direction I wanted to go, and life became relatively normal for a while. March passed, then April, and then May. Everyday was exactly the same: Work, sleep, drink, sleep, repeat. It was mostly a drama-free lifestyle; one that I'd wanted to live again for a while. As time went on though, my loneliness grew and my appetite for happiness and more became unsustainable. My drinking increased and I started smoking weed again almost everyday.

It was then that I saw it: a vision that threw me into a timeless panic.

I saw myself falling back down in the same hellhole of searching and addiction. I saw that my own choices and idolatries had led me through multiple detox units, two trips to rehab, two sober living programs, hundreds of A.A. meetings, multiple sponsors, and nearly a dozen doctors. Relapse after relapse, broken promises, and years of pain and regret. Rivers of tears, torn-apart relationships, self-mutilation, suicidal thinking, anxiety and depression. Vivid nightmares of the past, anger and rage and violence, heartbroken family members, and ruined dreams. And finally, this is what I had become — an empty, broken, humiliated piece of nothingness. I had hit my rock bottom. I had been humbled to the core and could no longer run away from the true solution. Deep down, I knew that in order to beat my addiction, I would have to submit to what I'd been running from.

Fourteen

My Christian background was always tangled up in my anxiety and addiction. Like many people raised in Christianity, I too had some weird and bad experiences with church that made me not want to go back. I wanted to feel normal, comfortable, and loved, but not at the cost of being turned into a miserable robot. To me, living life on a daily basis outside of church always felt much more normal. It was inside those walls that I felt fake and not myself. Let's not forget hypocrisy, but I wasn't old enough to even notice that. Feeling fake in itself was more than enough reason for me to not want to be involved with the church.

It would be unfair to put all of the blame on my church-going experiences, because I have always been the type of person that wanted to figure things out for himself and see what life had to offer, even if that meant learning the hard way. A lot of my rebellion was based on bitterness. I wanted to do things that I thought would lead me to happiness. I wanted to live my life in a way that completely pleased me. I wanted everything in life that opposed God.

Fast forward to my time in Atlanta.

During my time in Rod and Debra's program, I started listening to podcasts from a church in South Carolina that I actually enjoyed. I also began to read the Bible on my own accord. I needed to see for myself who God was and what Jesus was really like. What did He approve of and not approve of?

What did he love and what did he hate? Why should I even care? My intentions at the time were to fix my problem of hopelessness. I didn't care about doing anything for Jesus — I just wanted him to help me. It was a selfish decision; the best one I ever made.

The more time I invested in reading and listening, the clearer His message became to me; Jesus actually died for the idolater, the addict, and the hateful pagan like me. People like me were the ones who actually needed a Savior like Him. Jesus, who in my eyes had been fighting me, really wasn't. He *did* want to help me get out of my circumstances. It was myself who hadn't wanted to accept this truth. I didn't want to admit that it was my own pride and selfishness, my own *sin* that was causing me to chase this short-lived feeling of peace and happiness. It was me who wanted to please myself, live for myself, and run my life according to my own judgment. Look where that got me. The world told me that it was all about me and my happiness, but how is that true when nothing the world offered me could satisfy?

It takes a lot of pressure off of a person to realize that it's not all about them. No matter what you accomplish in your life, no matter how much money or power you have, no matter what wisdom you speak, you will die like everyone else and eventually be forgotten. It sounds depressing, but realizing that I existed for God, and not the other way around, provided much more hope and purpose. Life wasn't all about me, and thank God for that. In early June, I asked God for forgiveness from my self-seeking idolatry, and his help to stay sober. I was done running.

My life hardly changed overnight.

It was quite a slow process that was filled with mistakes, corrections and lessons. But, things did begin to get better; a small seed of faith had been planted.

The first positive change was my conscious choice to quit smoking weed — permanently. I had been sober from most of my drugs of choice for close to a year, but weed was still a big problem because it always led to more. An addict's advice rang in my head. "You have to want to stay sober just a little bit more than you want to use." On June 9th, I put that statement into practice and gutted through that first month without smoking any weed, which was far from enjoyable. Smoking weed made everything more fun, but it was a deceitful trick. The progress in overcoming my anxiety had become far too precious to me to continue down that road of denial. I knew that it made my anxiety far worse, so it had to be stopped.

The next change was my return to Greenville.

After spending exactly one year to the day in Atlanta, I moved back to South Carolina and enrolled in college again. The program of my choice was a two-year specialty degree that would prepare me to be certified as an occupational therapist assistant. But, before applying to this program, I had to take a lot of prerequisites to take; two years worth to be exact.

In previous years, many of my dollars and classes had been wasted by not appreciating the opportunity to learn, but that would not happen again. Books and knowledge that I once took for granted became gold to me. I tried to soak up as much of this information as possible. Academics, in a sense, became a new addiction, but a healthier one with promising outcomes. Exams were fun, going to class was fun, and learning new material was actually considered a privilege.

Another blessing was stopping the medicines that my body didn't need anymore. This too was a slow process, but those pills that I'd taken for years started to cause much more negative side-effects than positive ones. It was as if my brain decided for me that those medicines were no longer needed. The mood stabilizers were stopped, the sleeping medicines discontinued, and the anti-depressant greatly reduced. I started to become alive again. As a friend put it, "I became the old Zach again," with an elevated mood, increased energy, and the ability to feel raw emotion.

I felt invigorated, and my family was the first group of people to notice my change of heart and mind. The many years of dishonesty and manipulation had undoubtedly caused a lot of trust to be lost, but my family gave me a chance when I came home, and that's all I asked them for. It was difficult at first to remain patient, as I took on the task of winning back their trust. But whenever I would find myself becoming frustrated, I would simply put one of them in my own shoes. How would I act? How long would it take for one of them to regain my trust? Would I even speak to them anymore? The answer was never as gracious as the favor they were showing me. This in itself kept me humble and thankful.

Before I knew it, June had rolled back around and I had gone one year without marijuana or Klonopin. It had also been close to two years for opiates, and nearly three years for other substances. But, I had still not completely given up alcohol. I told many people that I was living sober and definitely bragged about it too. At the end of the day, it was my own denial that haunted me.

Truly, the obsession to stay drunk or high all the time was not driving me anymore. I didn't want that life. I was done with it, ready to pursue a newfound and much wiser path. *But why couldn't I settle down? Why did I still feel restless and antsy, and in need of a couple beers to relax?* There were times when I wouldn't drink for a week or two or three, but then the pressures of life would overwhelm me and I'd find myself cracking open a beer again. It bothered me, almost to the point of insanity. Many nights I would grind my teeth and mentally scream at myself.

You hypocrite!

- January 2014 -

I sat down one afternoon and began to write. It was one of the most spontaneous decisions I've ever made. There was no plan, no outline, and absolutely no previous thought about writing a book about my struggles — it just happened.

I downloaded a program on my computer and began to type my memory. The days turned to weeks, the weeks turned to months, and my writing slowly began to take shape. I enjoyed writing and the therapeutic rewards that it offered, but that wasn't my main purpose for writing. I wanted to believe that my story could provide hope to the people who struggle with addiction, anxiety, and depression. I wanted to share the hope that I had found through Jesus. How could I do this though, if I was still drinking?

My mind offered me an ultimatum: I could either dive in headfirst and totally commit to sobriety, or I could continue to neglect the tug on my soul to trust God and his plan for my life. After a couple more months, the tug of war became to great. I couldn't bathe in the lukewarm water any longer. It made me sick to my stomach.

It was October 2014. I was on a business trip with a friend in Baltimore. More or less, I was just the guy who went along to help out and give moral support. We decided to treat ourselves one night to an expensive seafood restaurant that was right on the harbor. It was a fantastic meal. I ordered clams, muscles, lobster claw, and other raw delicacies on the half-shell. I also had two glasses of red wine, *good* red wine. My vocabulary isn't strong enough to tell you how exactly how wonderful I felt. It was the best dinner I've ever had, and if it had been possible, I would have hit the pause button on that moment. It took every ounce of me to refrain from ordering another glass of red wine, and then another, and then another, and then another, until I blacked out.

I remember the moment vividly; when I knew that I was absolutely an alcoholic — a real alcoholic. Ironically, I was at complete peace with this realization. It was a different experience than the previous times when I had questioned my alcoholism. It was an intimate slice of time that I hope to never forget.

The following day, we drove down to D.C. for some sightseeing. It was October 8th. We stopped at an outside touristy type bar and each ordered our favorite kind of beer, an IPA. I stared at my glass for nearly thirty minutes. I may have had a sip or two, but that was it. My knees were weak and my mind was tired. All I could think about was that I didn't want to lose control anymore. I wanted to think clearly and speak wisely. I wanted to grow up and be a man. I needed peace.

My friend finished his beer, and we drove off. That was my last drink.

There were many times in the following months when I almost picked up a drink again. It was extremely difficult on the holidays, birthdays, and big social events where people tended to need a couple of drinks to loosen up anyway. However, I did not pick it up again. The stressful days came and went, emotionally exhausting days came and went, but I stayed sober and focused on the prize: One year sober. That's what I wanted, and the difficulty of achieving this goal made it that much more desirable to me. God's grace combined with perseverance gave me hope that it would happen. There were days when it was too much to bear, but that was when grace became real to me.

In the following year when I would run into people that only knew the old Zach, I could see the confusion in their eyes. They knew who I was, but they didn't *know* me anymore. I didn't like these encounters at first, but I grew to enjoy these random intimate moments as time passed. The conversation would always end up encouraging me to continue pursuing sobriety, and I always tried to be humble and give the glory to Jesus, because it truly is a miracle.

Even my old doctor didn't recognize his once shaky and pissed-off patient. He had seen me on and off since I was nineteen, but never before had I been able to speak with him about what caused my personal anxiety and cravings. Sometimes I could see that he didn't understand, but I think that was the spiritual aspect of my recovery. I saw him just about every three months, and each time I had become a little bit healthier and a little more secure in my sobriety.

- April 2015 -

It was time. I had completed all of the pre-requisites for the OTA program. The next step was to mail in my application. I was both nervous and excited, but I knew that five semesters worth of hard work would pay off.

In the last week of April, I sealed the envelope with all my paperwork and stuck it in the mail. It would take the college about six weeks to process my application and let me know if I was accepted in to the program. They said to expect a letter mid June. Honestly, I wasn't worried. My grades were solid and I had also completed a lot of bonus classes that would boost my chances.

This is what God wants me to do, right? He knows that I've fought hard to stay sober. He knows that I want to get a job and be successful. He knows that I'm trying.

From May to June, I worked six days a week and stayed as busy as possible. In fact, work was so slammed that I almost completely forgot about my application, at times. However, one night I had an extremely vivid dream where I got a letter back from the college stating that I hadn't been accepted to the program.

The dream stuck with me, and I remember being angry about it because I knew it was true. I suppose that's why it wasn't a shock to me when I *did* get a letter in the mail, which stated that I had *not* been accepted into the program. No, it wasn't shocking news, but it still stung. I felt purposeless, use-less, and once again like a failure. All the time and hard work seemed to have been wasted. *Why had I felt so strongly that I was supposed to go back to Greenville and enroll in school? What am I sup-posed to do now?* I put my head in my hands with the letter and began to cry; it all started to come out. As I sat there in tears, I could feel God telling me that He had better plans for me. I didn't know what they were, but I repeated it over and over to myself.

The next day I picked myself back up and went to work. I stayed as busy as possible with my job. I worked six days a week during the summer, packing and unloading trucks from house to house. Everyday was different, challenging, and full of surprises. It was by far the most physically demanding job that I've ever had, but all of the strenuous labor seemed to click with my daily sobriety. At the end of the day when I would be physically beat down and exhausted, I would also be mentally serene. I would come home with a clear mind, com-pletely content with a bed and a pillow. There were days when I swore under my breath that I would drink work, but these stressful moments would always fizzle out by the end of the job. I was always able to find humor in my least serine mo-ments.

Fifteen

It's time to switch to the present.

It's Sunday night, and tomorrow I'm going to wake up and move some furniture from house to house. I don't foresee this being my permanent career, but right now this is where God wants me to be. I'm not certain about a lot of things right now, but what I am certain about is this: I am healthy, I have a well-paying job, food, a car, a savings account, friends and family that love me, and most importantly, a Savior that has my trust. I am so blessed.

That doesn't mean I don't ask questions. I definitely do. I'f I could sit down right now and talk with Jesus, I would ask for some clarity on more than a few things. I would tell Him that I don't want to be a bitter addict, full of anger towards the world because I cannot drink alcohol. I would tell Him that I don't want to be self-righteous and judge-mental towards people who can drink. I want to remain humble and broken, full of forgiveness and love for everyone. This was the hand I was dealt, and to not acknowledge my thousands of other blessings would label me as a fool. Addiction is a disease, but to simply label it as such would be only partially true. Addiction is also a heart issue.

Guilt and shame was a big distraction in my recovery for the first year that I was back in Greenville. I knew that Jesus had given me a clean slate and that I was forgiven, but unless I constantly reminded myself of this, my past tended to steal my daily joy. But, I am a new person and dwelling on the past is not what God wants for me.

I never elaborated how my anxiety grew to be as bad as it was. When I was little, I always remember being scared and worried about things, but I thought that was normal. I remember being eleven or twelve years old and playing a baseball game. My parents said that they were going to be there, but when the game started and my mom was not in the stands, I started to worry. Then I heard a siren and assumed that she had been in an accident. I may be wrong, but I'm sure that most twelve year olds do not concern themselves with thoughts like these, especially during a baseball game. I was so nervous that I could barely play. That's one example, but I feel that it gives you an idea about the nervous disposition I had while growing up.

I started taking amphetamines in middle school to help with my focusing and hyperactivity. That led to my brain racing even faster, which led to me needing something to turn off my thinking, hence marijuana. Marijuana led to other things, other things led to more things, and more things led to the beginning of my story. The point is — over the years my anxiety got worse and worse, and I always thought that the drugs and alcohol were alleviating it. What I didn't know was that they made everything far worse. It was one hell of a cycle, and I believe that's one of the reasons why I got into drugs and alcohol so bad.

Nowadays, my anxiety has been reduced to the point that, on most days, I completely forget what *true* anxiety feels like. Anxiety that won't allow me to leave the house. Anxiety that disorients me beyond belief. Anxiety that cripples my personality and distorts my motivation. All of that is gone, and I am so blessed for that. I hope to never take a worry-free day for granted.

Every now and again I'll have a bad day, but I consider these days blessings too, as they remind me of how far I've come and how much I still need God's grace.

Throughout most of my writing process, I planned on ending strongly enough to not have any doubts on my own sobriety. I planned on being a bit further on in my quest of life, and I planned on being certain about my future. But, as time as gone on and I've continued to write, it appears that I'm not as secure in my sobriety as I once thought. I'm still fighting everyday to stay on a path that won't lead me back to where I started from. Obsessions and cravings do not consume me anymore, but I do have days where staying sober is the last thing I want to do. There have been multiple times when all I've wanted to do is set my computer on fire and completely forget about this book and everything that I went through to learn about myself, who I am, and what I believe in.

The choice is so easy, yet it is a constant part of my life. All I have to do is say NO everyday, and I will continue to grow in ways that I didn't think would be possible. Staying sober has allowed me to succeed in every single aspect of my life. From conflicts to stress, success to failure, and all the emotional colors in-between — I've changed.

I can look myself in mirror and be proud of who I am. While I haven't relapsed from substances, I do fall short of character perfection everyday. I think that's why the tone of my book is going to end in a different way than I imagined.

Staying sober is just one aspect of life, and the life of an addict is much more important than just living sober.

I want you to know that I don't hate alcoholics anonymous, although I understand why it may look that way at times. The truth is this: A.A. is a great program and it *does* provide a way for the addict and alcoholic to get and stay sober. I've met many of these addicts and I've seen it work. A.A. has always welcomed me no matter how messed up I was when I walked through the doors. I will still go to meetings and use the tools A.A. provides, but my ultimate peace resides only in Jesus Christ. I choose to put my hope in a completely perfect Savior, who will never let me down.

I give complete glory to Jesus and everything he has blessed me with, including a brain and daily desire to seek healthier remedies for dealing with anxiety and addiction. Out of all the techniques, pills, and therapies, physical activity and daily exercise has been the most rewarding to me. It helps me get out of my head and resets my thinking. It's why I'm completely satisfied with my physically exhausting job, and it's why I'm back in the weight room again.

While I cannot speak for everyone, I believe that deep down every addict is searching for the high that will never leave them. I believe that every addict wants something that will end the cravings, the longing, and the lack of purpose. If an addict were to ask me why they should follow Jesus, I would tell them that He fills that void. He is the cure to the daily pursuit of more. It may not take place instantly, but if you *truly* want to get out of the hell that you are in, I know without a shadow of a doubt that He can rescue you.

While I've never read the Bible and felt as physically good as

I did on drugs, I do know that the satisfaction from Jesus is a much better high to seek. Instant gratification does not allow for growth, but running the race and fighting the fight produces true character.

I didn't write down the last thing that Rod in Atlanta told me. We were talking about Christians and he said, "You know what Gandhi said about Jesus? He said that Christians are nothing like their Jesus." I thought about what Rod said for a year straight, probably because he is right. We are nothing like Jesus, but that's why we need Him so much. Nobody always practices what they preach, but that's because they are human, and that's we need a perfect Savior like Jesus. Christians are never going to be sinless, but true followers of Christ are well aware of this and don't try to morally place themselves on the top shelf.

It's been just over two years since I started writing my story. It feels like a long time, but it also feels like just yesterday that I sat down with my dad and casually mentioned that I was going to write a book. It has been a long writing process that has proved to be more than beneficial. I forced myself to be patient, and that has allowed me to grow tremendously throughout the process. The writing is therapeutic in itself, and I will continue to pursue writing long after completing this story.

It's now time to move on, but part of me is scared to do so because like most everything else, I've grown comfortable in my routine. I still don't love change, but change is what got me to where I am today, and change will get me to where I need to be.

If you are an addict struggling with sobriety, just know that I am too. I understand completely how you feel. I know what it's like to crawl on your hands and knees searching through dust and dirt to find the smallest flakes of that next high. I know what it's like to have friends die from addiction. I know what it's like to not want to live anymore. I know what it's like to scream and kick and fight and cry out in pain. I know what it's like to be in a bubble of personal anguish and hell. But, I also know what it's like to surrender. I know what it's like to finally cry out to God and ask for help — true and pure help. I know what it's like to make a choice to stay sober for one hour at a time. I know what it's like to be secure, and I know what it's like to have hope.

I know what it can be like on the other side.

ACKNOWLEDGEMENTS

A very special thanks to my editor David, and my designer Neil. I couldn't have done it without you guys. Thank you Dan and Andrew for your insight and advice.

Made in the USA
San Bernardino, CA
21 July 2016